MY FAVORITE CAKES

2021

FLAVORFUL RECIPES FOR EVERY OCCASION

KATE LAMPARD

Table of Contents

Custard Tarts

Makes 12

225 g/8 oz Shortcrust Pastry

15 ml/1 tbsp caster (superfine) sugar

1 egg, lightly beaten

150 ml/¼ pt/2/3 cup warm milk

A pinch of salt

Grated nutmeg for sprinkling

Roll out the pastry and use to line 12 deep tartlet tins (patty pans). Mix the sugar into the egg, then gradually stir in the warm milk and salt. Pour the mixture into the pastry cases (pie shells) and sprinkle with nutmeg. Bake in a preheated oven at 200°C/400°F/gas mark 6 for 20 minutes. Leave to cool in the tins.

Danish Custard Tartlets

Makes 8

200 g/7 oz/scant 1 cup butter or margarine

250 g/9 oz/2¼ cups plain (all-purpose) flour

50 g/2 oz/1/3 cup icing (confectioners') sugar, sifted

2 egg yolks

1 quantity Danish Custard Filling

Rub the butter or margarine into the flour and sugar until the mixture resembles breadcrumbs. Work in the egg yolks until well blended. Cover with clingfilm (plastic wrap) and chill for 1 hour. Roll out two-thirds of the pastry (paste) and use to line greased tartlet tins (patty pans). Fill with the custard filling. Roll out the remaining pastry and cut out lids for the tarts. Moisten the edges and press them together to seal. Bake in a preheated oven at 200°C/400°F/gas mark 6 for 15–20 minutes until golden. Leave to cool in the tins.

Fruit Tartlets

Makes 12

75 g/3 oz/1/3 cup butter or margarine, diced

175 g/6 oz/1½ cups plain (all-purpose) flour

45 ml/3 tbsp caster (superfine) sugar

10 ml/2 tsp finely grated orange rind

1 egg yolk

15 ml/1 tbsp water

175 g/6 oz/¾ cup cream cheese

15 ml/1 tbsp milk

350 g/12 oz mixed fruit such as halved seedless grapes, mandarin segments, sliced strawberries, blackberries or raspberries

45 ml/3 tbsp apricot jam (conserve), sieved (strained)

15 ml/1 tbsp water

Rub the butter or margarine into the flour until the mixture resembles breadcrumbs. Stir in 30 ml/2 tbsp of the sugar and half the orange rind. Add the egg yolk and just enough of the water to mix to a soft dough. Wrap in clingfilm (plastic wrap) and chill for 30 minutes.

Roll out the pastry (paste) to 3mm/ 1/8 in thick on a lightly floured surface and use to line 12 barquette (boat-shaped) or tartlet moulds. Cover with greaseproof (waxed) paper, fill with baking beans and bake in a preheated oven at 190°C/ 375°F/gas mark 5 for 10 minutes. Remove the paper and beans and bake for a further 5 minutes until golden. Leave to cool in the tins for 5 minutes, then turn out on to a wire rack to finish cooling.

Beat the cheese with the milk, the remaining sugar and orange rind until smooth. Spoon into the pastry cases (pie shells) and arrange the fruit on top. Heat the jam and water in a small pan until well blended, then brush over the fruit to glaze. Chill before serving.

Genoese Tart

Makes one 23 cm/9 in tart

100 g/4 oz Puff Pastry

50 g/2 oz/¼ cup butter or margarine, softened

75 g/3 oz/1/3 cup caster (superfine) sugar

75 g/3 oz/¾ cup almonds, chopped

3 eggs, separated

2.5 ml/½ tsp vanilla essence (extract)

100 g/4 oz/1 cup plain (all-purpose) flour

100 g/4 oz/2/3 cup icing (confectioners') sugar, sifted

Juice of ½ lemon

Roll out the pastry on a lightly floured surface and use to line a 23 cm/9 in cake tin (pan). Prick all over with a fork. Cream together the butter or margarine and caster sugar until light and fluffy. Gradually beat in the almonds, egg yolks and vanilla essence. Fold in the flour. Beat the egg whites until stiff, then fold into the mixture. Spoon into the pastry case (pie shell) and bake in a preheated oven at 190°C/375°F/gas mark 5 for 30 minutes. Allow to cool for 5 minutes. Blend the icing sugar with the lemon juice and spread over the top of the tart.

Ginger Tart

Makes one 23 cm/9 in tart

225 g/8 oz/2/3 cup golden (light corn) syrup

250 ml/8 fl oz/1 cup boiling water

2.5 ml/½ tsp ground ginger

60 ml/4 tbsp finely chopped crystallised (candied) ginger

30 ml/2 tbsp cornflour (cornstarch)

15 ml/1 tbsp custard powder

1 Basic Sponge Tart Case

Bring the syrup, water and ground ginger to the boil, then stir in the crystallised ginger. Mix together the cornflour and custard powder to a paste with a little water, then stir it into the ginger mixture and cook over a low heat for a few minutes, stirring continuously. Spoon the filling into the tart case (shell) and leave to cool and set.

Jam Tarts

Makes 12

225 g/8 oz Shortcrust Pastry

175 g/6 oz/½ cup firm or whole fruit jam (conserve)

Roll out the pastry (paste) and use to line a greased bun tin (patty pan). Divide the jam between the tarts and bake in a preheated oven at 200°C/400°F/gas mark 6 for 15 minutes.

Pecan Tart

Makes one 23 cm/9 in tart

225 g/8 oz Shortcrust Pastry

50 g/2 oz/½ cup pecan nuts

3 eggs

225 g/8 oz/2/3 cup golden (light corn) syrup

75 g/3 oz/1/3 cup soft brown sugar

2.5 ml/½ tsp vanilla essence (extract)

A pinch of salt

Roll out the pastry (paste) on a lightly floured surface and use to line a greased 23 cm/9 in flan dish. Cover with greaseproof (waxed) paper, fill with baking beans and bake blind in a preheated oven at 190°C/375°F/gas mark 5 for 10 minutes. Remove the paper and beans.

Arrange the pecans in an attractive pattern in the pastry case (pie shell). Beat the eggs until light and frothy. Beat in the syrup, then the sugar and continue beating until the sugar has dissolved. Add the vanilla essence and salt and beat until smooth. Spoon the mixture into the case and bake in the preheated oven for 10 minutes. Reduce the oven temperature to 180°C/350°F/gas mark 4 and bake for a further 30 minutes until golden. Leave to cool and set before serving.

Pecan and Apple Tart

Makes one 23 cm/9 in tart

2 eggs

350 g/12 oz/1½ cups caster (superfine) sugar

50 g/2 oz/½ cup plain (all-purpose) flour

10 ml/2 tsp baking powder

A pinch of salt

100 g/4 oz cooking (tart) apples, peeled, cored and diced

100 g/4 oz/1 cup pecan nuts or walnuts

150 ml/¼ pt/2/3 cup whipped cream

Beat the eggs until pale and frothy. Stir in all the remaining ingredients, except the cream, one at a time in the order listed. Spoon into a greased and lined 23 cm/9 in cake tin (pan) and bake in a preheated oven at 160°C/325°F/ gas 3 for about 45 minutes until well risen and golden brown. Serve with the cream.

Gainsborough Tart

Makes one 20 cm/8 in tart

25 g/1 oz/2 tbsp butter or margarine

2.5 ml/½ tsp baking powder

50 g/2 oz/¼ cup caster (superfine) sugar

100 g/4 oz/1 cup desiccated (shredded) coconut

50 g/2 oz/¼ cup glacé (candied) cherries, chopped

2 eggs, beaten

Melt the butter, then mix in the remaining ingredients and spoon into a greased and lined 20 cm/8 in cake tin (pan). Bake in a preheated oven at 180°C/350°F/gas mark 4 for 30 minutes until springy to the touch.

Lemon Tart

Makes one 25 cm/10 in tart

225 g/8 oz Shortcrust Pastry

100 g/4 oz/½ cup butter or margarine

4 eggs

Grated rind and juice of 2 lemons

100 g/4 oz/½ cup caster (superfine) sugar

250 ml/8 fl oz/1 cup double (heavy) cream

Mint leaves to decorate

Roll out the pastry (paste) on a lightly floured surface and use to line a 25 cm/10 in flan tin (pan). Prick the base with a fork. Cover with greaseproof (waxed) paper and fill with baking beans. Bake in a preheated oven at 200°C/ 400°F/gas mark 6 for 10 minutes. Remove the paper and beans and return to the oven for a further 5 minutes until the base is dry. Reduce the oven temperature to 160°C/325°F/gas mark 3.

Melt the butter or margarine, then leave to cool for 1 minute. Whisk the eggs with the lemon rind and juice. Whisk in the butter, sugar and cream. Pour into the pastry base and bake at the reduced temperature for 20 minutes. Leave to cool, then chill before serving, decorated with mint leaves.

Lemon Tartlets

Makes 12

225 g/8 oz/1 cup butter or margarine, softened

75 g/3 oz/½ cup icing (confectioners') sugar, sifted

175 g/6 oz/1½ cups plain (all-purpose) flour

50 g/2 oz/½ cup cornflour (cornstarch)

5 ml/1 tsp grated lemon rind

For the topping:

30 ml/2 tbsp lemon curd

30 ml/2 tbsp icing (confectioners') sugar, sifted

Blend together all the cake ingredients until soft. Spoon into a piping bag and pipe decoratively into 12 paper cases placed in a bun tin (patty pan). Bake in a preheated oven at 180°C/350°F/gas mark 4 for 20 minutes until pale golden. Leave to cool slightly, then place a spoonful of lemon curd on top of each cake and dust with icing sugar.

Orange Tart

Makes one 23 cm/9 in tart

1 Basic Sponge Tart Case

400 ml/14 fl oz/1¾ cups orange juice

150 g/5 oz/2/3 cup caster (superfine) sugar

30 ml/2 tbsp custard powder

15 g/½ oz/1 tbsp butter or margarine

15 ml/1 tbsp grated orange rind

A few candied orange slices (optional)

Prepare the basic sponge tart case (shell). While it is cooking, mix 250 ml/8 fl oz/1 cup of the orange juice with the sugar, custard powder and butter or margarine. Bring the mixture to the boil over a low heat and simmer gently until transparent and thick. Stir in the orange rind. As soon as the flan case comes out of the oven, spoon over the remaining orange juice, then spoon the orange filling into the flan and leave to cool and set. Decorate with candied orange slices, if liked.

Pear Tart

Makes one 20 cm/8 in tart

1 quantity Pâte Sucrée

For the filling:

150 ml/¼ pt/2/3 cup double (heavy) cream

2 eggs

50 g/2 oz/¼ cup caster (superfine) sugar

5 pears

For the glaze:

75 ml/5 tbsp redcurrant jelly (clear conserve)

30 ml/2 tbsp water

A squeeze of lemon juice

Roll out the pâte sucrée and use to line a 20 cm/8 in flan tin (pan). Cover with greaseproof (waxed) paper and fill with baking beans and bake in a preheated oven at 190°C/375°F/gas mark 5 for 12 minutes. Remove from the oven, remove the paper and beans and leave to cool.

To make the filling, mix together the cream, eggs and sugar. Peel and core the pears and cut in half lengthways. Place cut side down and slice almost through to the centre of the pears, but still leaving them intact. Arrange in the tart case (shell). Pour over the cream mixture and bake in a preheated oven at 190°C/375°F/gas mark 4 for 45 minutes, covering with greaseproof (waxed) paper if it browns before the cream is set. Leave to cool.

To make the glaze, melt the jelly, water and lemon juice in a small pan until blended. Brush over the fruit while the glaze is hot, then leave to set. Serve the same day.

Pear and Almond Tart

Makes one 20 cm/8 in tart

For the pastry (paste):

100 g/4 oz/1 cup plain (all-purpose) flour

50 g/2 oz/½ cup ground almonds

50 g/2 oz/¼ cup caster (superfine) sugar

75 g/3 oz/1/3 cup butter or margarine, diced and softened

1 egg yolk

A few drops of almond essence (extract)

For the filling:

1 egg yolk

50 g/2 oz/¼ cup caster (superfine) sugar

50 g/2 oz/½ cup ground almonds

30 ml/2 tbsp pear-flavoured liqueur or other liqueur to taste

3 large pears

For the custard:

3 eggs

25 g/1 oz/2 tbsp caster (superfine) sugar

300 ml/½ pt/1¼ cups single (light) cream

To make the pastry, mix together the flour, almonds and sugar in a bowl and make a well in the centre. Add the butter or margarine, egg yolk and vanilla essence and gradually work the ingredients together until you have a soft dough. Wrap in clingfilm (plastic wrap) and chill for 45 minutes. Roll out on a floured surface and use to line a greased and lined 20 cm/8 in flan tin (pan). Cover with greaseproof (waxed) paper and fill with baking beans and bake blind in a preheated oven at 200°C/400°F/gas mark 6 for 15 minutes. Remove the paper and beans.

To make the filling, beat together the egg yolk and sugar. Stir in the almonds and liqueur and spoon the mixture into the pastry case (pie shell). Peel, core and halve the pears, then arrange them flat side down on the filling.

To make the custard, beat together the eggs and sugar until pale and fluffy. Stir in the cream. Cover the pears with the custard and bake in a preheated oven at 180°C/350°F/gas mark 4 for about 15 minutes until the custard is just set.

Royal Raisin Tart

Makes one 20 cm/8 in tart

For the pastry (paste):

100 g/4 oz/½ cup butter or margarine

225 g/8 oz/2 cups plain (all-purpose) flour

A pinch of salt

45 ml/3 tbsp cold water

For the filling:

50 g/2 oz/½ cup cake crumbs

175 g/6 oz/1 cup raisins

1 egg yolk

5 ml/1 tsp grated lemon rind

For the topping:

225 g/8 oz/11/3 cups icing (confectioners') sugar, sifted

1 egg white

5 ml/1 tsp lemon juice

To finish:

45 ml/3 tbsp redcurrant jelly (clear conserve)

To make the pastry, rub the butter or margarine into the flour and salt until the mixture resembles breadcrumbs. Mix in enough cold water to make a pastry. Wrap in clingfilm (plastic wrap) and chill for 30 minutes.

Roll out the pastry and use to line a 20 cm/8 in square cake tin (pan). Mix together the filling ingredients and spoon over the base, levelling the top. Beat the topping ingredients together and spread over the cake. Beat the redcurrant jelly until smooth, then pipe a trellis design over the top of the cake. Bake in a preheated oven at 190°C/375°F/gas mark 5 for 30 minutes, then reduce the oven temperature to 180°C/350°F/gas mark 4 and bake for a further 10 minutes.

Raisin and Soured Cream Tart

Makes one 23 cm/9 in tart

225 g/8 oz Shortcrust Pastry

30 ml/2 tbsp plain (all-purpose) flour

2 eggs, lightly beaten

60 ml/4 tbsp caster (superfine) sugar

250 ml/8 fl oz/1 cup soured (dairy sour) cream

225 g/8 oz/11/3 cups raisins

60 ml/4 tbsp rum or brandy

A few drops of vanilla essence (extract)

Roll out the pastry (paste) to 5mm/¼ in thick on a lightly floured surface. Mix together the flour, eggs, sugar and cream, then stir in the raisins, rum or brandy and vanilla essence. Spoon the mixture into the pastry case and bake in a preheated oven at 200°C/400°F/gas mark 6 for 20 minutes. Reduce the oven temperature to 180°C/350°F/gas mark 4 and bake for a further 5 minutes until just set.

Strawberry Tart

Makes one 20 cm/8 in tart

1 quantity Pâte Sucrée

For the filling:

5 egg yolks

175 g/6 oz/¾ cup caster (superfine) sugar

75 g/3 oz/¾ cup cornflour (cornstarch)

1 vanilla pod (bean)

450 ml/¾ pt/2 cups milk

15 g/½ oz/1 tbsp butter or margarine

550 g/1¼ lb strawberries, halved

For the glaze:

75 ml/5 tbsp redcurrant jelly (clear conserve)

30 ml/2 tbsp water

A squeeze of lemon juice

Roll out the pastry (paste) and use to line a 20 cm/8 in flan tin (pan). Cover with greaseproof (waxed) paper and fill with baking beans and bake in a preheated oven at 190°C/375°F/gas mark 5 for 12 minutes. Remove from the oven, remove the paper and beans and leave to cool.

To make the filling, beat together the egg yolks and sugar until the mixture is pale and fluffy and trails from the whisk in ribbons. Beat in the cornflour. Place the vanilla pod in the milk and bring to the boil. Remove the vanilla pod. Gradually beat into the egg mixture. Pour the mixture into a clean pan and bring to the boil, stirring continuously, then cook, still stirring, for 3 minutes. Remove from the heat and stir in the butter or margarine until melted. Cover with buttered greaseproof (waxed) paper and leave to cool.

Spoon the custard into the pastry case (pie shell) and arrange the strawberries attractively on the top. To make the glaze, melt the jelly, water and lemon juice until blended. Brush over the fruit while the glaze is hot, then leave to set. Serve the same day.

Treacle Tart

Makes one 20 cm/8 in tart

75 g/3 oz/1/3 cup butter or margarine

175 g/6 oz/1½ cups plain (all-purpose) flour

15 ml/1 tbsp caster (superfine) sugar

1 egg yolk

30 ml/2 tbsp water

225 g/8 oz/2/3 cup golden (light corn) syrup

50 g/2 oz/1 cup fresh breadcrumbs

5 ml/1 tsp lemon juice

Rub the butter or margarine into the flour until the mixture resembles breadcrumbs. Stir in the sugar, then add the egg yolk and water and mix to a pastry (paste). Wrap in clingfilm (plastic wrap) and chill for 30 minutes.

Roll out the pastry and use to line a 20 cm/8 in flan tin (pan). Warm the syrup, then mix it with the breadcrumbs and lemon juice. Spoon the filling into the pastry case and bake in a preheated oven at 180°C/350°F/gas mark 4 for 35 minutes until bubbling.

Walnut and Treacle Tart

Makes one 20 cm/8 in tart

225 g/8 oz Shortcrust Pastry

100 g/4 oz/½ cup butter or margarine, softened

50 g/2 oz/¼ cup soft brown sugar

2 eggs, beaten

175 g/6 oz/½ cup golden (light corn) syrup, warmed

100 g/4 oz/1 cup walnuts, finely chopped

Grated rind of 1 lemon

Juice of ½ lemon

Roll out the pastry (paste) and use to line a greased 20 cm/8 in cake tin (pan). Cover with greaseproof (waxed) paper and fill with baking beans and bake in a preheated oven at 200°C/400°F/gas mark 6 for 10 minutes. Remove from the oven and remove the paper and beans. Reduce the oven temperature to 180°C/350°F/gas mark 4.

Beat together the butter or margarine and sugar until pale and fluffy. Gradually beat in the eggs, then stir in the syrup, walnuts, lemon rind and juice. Spoon into the pastry case (pie shell) and bake in the oven for 45 minutes until browned and crisp.

Amish Shoo-fly Cake

Makes one 23 x 30 cm cake

225 g/8 oz/1 cup butter or margarine, softened

225 g/8 oz/2 cups plain (all-purpose) flour

225 g/8 oz/2 cups wholemeal (wholewheat) flour

450 g/1 lb/2 cups soft brown sugar

350 g/12 oz/1 cup black treacle (molasses)

10 ml/2 tsp bicarbonate of soda (baking soda)

450 ml/¾ pt/2 cups boiling water

Rub the butter or margarine into the flours until the mixture resembles breadcrumbs. Stir in the sugar. Set aside 100 g/4 oz/1 cup of the mixture for the topping. Mix together the treacle, bicarbonate of soda and water and stir into the flour mixture just until the dry ingredients have been absorbed. Spoon into a greased and floured 23 x 30 cm/9 x 12 in cake tin (pan) and sprinkle with the reserved mixture. Bake in a preheated oven at 180°C/350°F/gas mark 4 for 35 minutes until a skewer inserted in the centre comes out clean. Serve warm.

Boston Custard Slice

Makes one 23 cm/9 in cake

100 g/4 oz/½ cup butter or margarine, softened

225 g/8 oz/1 cup caster (superfine) sugar

2 eggs, lightly beaten

2.5 ml/½ tsp vanilla essence (extract)

175 g/6 oz/1½ cups self-raising (self-rising) flour

5 ml/1 tsp baking powder

A pinch of salt

60 ml/4 tbsp milk

Custard Filling

Cream together the butter or margarine and sugar until light and fluffy. Gradually add the eggs and vanilla essence, beating well after each addition. Mix together the flour, baking powder and salt and add to the mixture alternately with the milk. Spoon into a greased and floured 23 cm/9 in cake tin (pan) and bake in a preheated oven at 180°C/350°F/gas mark 4 for 30 minutes until firm to the touch. When cool, cut the cake horizontally and sandwich the two halves together with the custard filling.

American White Mountain Cake

Makes one 23 cm/9 in cake

225 g/8 oz/1 cup butter or margarine, softened

450 g/1 lb/2 cups caster (superfine) sugar

3 eggs, lightly beaten

350 g/12 oz/3 cups self-raising (self-rising) flour

15 ml/1 tbsp baking powder

1.5 ml/¼ tsp salt

250 ml/8 fl oz/1 cup milk

5 ml/1 tsp vanilla essence (extract)

5 ml/1 tsp almond essence (extract)

For the lemon filling:
45 ml/3 tbsp cornflour (cornstarch)

75 g/3 oz/1/3 cup caster (superfine) sugar

1.5 ml/¼ tsp salt

300 ml/½ pt/1¼ cups milk

25 g/1 oz/2 tbsp butter or margarine

90 ml/6 tbsp lemon juice

5 ml/1 tsp grated lemon rind

For the frosting:
350 g/12 oz/1½ cups caster (superfine) sugar

A pinch of salt

2 egg whites

75 ml/5 tbsp cold water

15 ml/1 tbsp golden (light corn) syrup

5 ml/1 tsp vanilla essence (extract)

175 g/6 oz/1½ cups desiccated (shredded) coconut

Cream together the butter or margarine and sugar until light and fluffy. Gradually beat in the eggs. Mix together the flour, baking powder and salt, then add to the creamed mixture alternately with the milk and essences. Spoon the mixture into three greased and lined 23 cm/9 in cake tins (pans) and bake in a preheated oven at 180°C/350°F/gas mark 4 for 30 minutes until a skewer inserted into the centre comes out clean. Leave to cool.

To make the filling, mix together the cornflour, sugar and salt, then whisk in the milk until blended. Add the butter or margarine in pieces and whisk over a low heat for about 2 minutes until thick. Stir in the lemon juice and rind. Leave to cool and chill.

To make the frosting, mix together all the ingredients except the vanilla essence and coconut in a heatproof bowl set over a pan of gently simmering water. Beat for about 5 minutes until stiff. Stir in the vanilla essence and beat for a further 2 minutes.

To assemble the cake, spread the base layer with half the lemon filling and sprinkle with 25 g/1 oz/¼ cup of coconut. Repeat with the second layer. Spread the frosting over the top and sides of the cake and sprinkle with the remaining coconut.

American Buttermilk Cake

Makes one 23 cm/9 in cake

100 g/4 oz/½ cup butter or margarine, softened

225 g/8 oz/1 cup caster (superfine) sugar

2 eggs, lightly beaten

5 ml/1 tsp grated lemon rind

5 ml/1 tsp vanilla essence (extract)

225 g/8 oz/2 cups self-raising (self-rising) flour

5 ml/1 tsp baking powder

5 ml/1 tsp bicarbonate of soda (baking soda)

A pinch of salt

250 ml/8 fl oz/1 cup buttermilk

Lemon Filling

Cream together the butter or margarine and sugar until light and fluffy. Gradually beat in the eggs, then stir in the lemon rind and vanilla essence. Mix together the flour, baking powder, bicarbonate of soda and salt and add to the mixture alternately with the buttermilk. Beat well until smooth. Spoon the mixture into two greased and floured 23 cm/9 in cake tins (pans) and bake in a preheated oven at 180°C/350°F/gas mark 4 for 25 minutes until firm to the touch. Leave to cool in the tins for 5 minutes before turning out on to a wire rack to finish cooling. When cool, sandwich together with the lemon filling.

Caribbean Ginger and Rum Cake

Makes one 20 cm/8 in cake

50 g/2 oz/¼ cup butter or margarine

120 ml/4 fl oz/½ cup black treacle (molasses)

1 egg, lightly beaten

60 ml/4 tbsp rum

100 g/4 oz/1 cup self-raising (self-rising) flour

10 ml/2 tsp ground ginger

75 g/3 oz/1/3 cup soft brown sugar

25 g/1 oz crystallised (candied) ginger, chopped

Melt the butter or margarine with the treacle over a low heat, then leave to cool slightly. Stir in the remaining ingredients to make a soft batter. Spoon into a greased and lined 20 cm/8 in ring tin (pan) and bake in a preheated oven at 200°C/400°F/gas mark 6 for 20 minutes until well risen and firm to the touch.

Sachertorte

Makes one 20 cm/8 in cake

200 g/7 oz/1¾ cups plain (semi-sweet) chocolate

8 eggs, separated

100 g/4 oz/½ cup unsalted (sweet) butter, melted

2 egg whites

A pinch of salt

150 g /5 oz/2/3 cup caster (superfine) sugar

A few drops of vanilla essence (extract)

100 g/4 oz/1 cup plain (all-purpose) flour

For the icing (frosting):

150 g/5 oz/1¼ cups plain (semi-sweet) chocolate

250 ml/8 fl oz/1 cup single (light) cream

175 g/6 oz/¾ cup caster (superfine) sugar

A few drops of vanilla essence (extract)

1 egg, beaten

100 g/4 oz/1/3 cup apricot jam (conserve), sieved (strained)

Melt the chocolate in a heatproof bowl set over a pan of gently simmering water. Remove from the heat. Lightly beat the egg yolks with the butter, then stir into the melted chocolate. Whisk all the egg whites and the salt until stiff, then gradually add the sugar and vanilla essence and continue to beat until the mixture stands in stiff peaks. Gradually fold into the chocolate mixture, then fold in the flour. Spoon the mixture into two greased and lined 20 cm/8 in cake tins (pans) and bake in a preheated oven at 180°C/350°F/gas mark 4 for 45 minutes until a skewer inserted in the centre comes out clean. Turn out on to a wire rack and leave to cool.

To make the icing, melt the chocolate with the cream, sugar and vanilla essence over a medium heat until well blended, then simmer for 5 minutes without stirring. Mix a few spoonfuls of the chocolate mixture with the egg, then stir into the chocolate and cook for 1 minute, stirring. Remove from the heat and leave to cool to room temperature.

Sandwich the cakes together with the apricot jam. Cover the whole cake with the chocolate icing, smoothing the surface with a palette knife or spatula. Leave to cool, then chill for several hours until the icing hardens.

Caribbean Rum Fruit Cake

Makes one 20 cm/8 in cake

450 g/1 lb/22/3 cups dried mixed fruit (fruit cake mix)

225 g/8 oz/11/3 cups sultanas (golden raisins)

100 g/4 oz/2/3 cup raisins

100 g/4 oz/2/3 cup currants

50 g/2 oz/¼ cup glacé (candied) cherries

300 ml/½ pt/1¼ cups red wine

225 g/8 oz/1 cup butter or margarine, softened

225 g/8 oz/1 cup soft brown sugar

5 eggs, lightly beaten

10 ml/2 tsp black treacle (molasses)

225 g/8 oz/2 cups plain (all-purpose) flour

50 g/2 oz/½ cup ground almonds

5 ml/1 tsp ground cinnamon

5 ml/1 tsp grated nutmeg

5 ml/1 tsp vanilla essence (extract)

300 ml/½ pt/1¼ cups rum

Place all the fruit and the wine in a pan and bring to the boil. Reduce the heat to minimum, cover and leave for 15 minutes, then remove from the heat and leave to cool. Cream together the butter or margarine and sugar until light and fluffy, then gradually mix in the eggs and treacle. Fold in the dry ingredients. Stir in the fruit mixture, vanilla essence and 45 ml/ 3 tbsp of the rum. Spoon into a greased and lined 20 cm/8 in cake tin (pan) and bake in a preheated oven at 160°C/325°F/ gas mark 3 for 3 hours until well risen and a skewer inserted in the centre comes out clean. Leave to cool in the tin for 10 minutes, then turn out on to a wire rack to finish cooling. Pierce the top of the cake with a fine skewer and spoon over the remaining rum. Wrap in foil and leave to mature for as long as possible.

Danish Butter Cake

Makes one 23 cm/9 in cake

225 g/8 oz/1 cup butter or margarine, diced

175 g/6 oz/1½ cups plain (all-purpose) flour

40 g/1½ oz fresh yeast or 60 ml/4 tbsp dried yeast

15 ml/1 tbsp granulated sugar

1 egg, beaten

½ quantity Danish Custard Filling

60 ml/4 tbsp icing (confectioners') sugar, sifted

45 ml/3 tbsp currants

Rub 100 g/4 oz/½ cup of the butter or margarine into the flour. Cream together the yeast and granulated sugar, then add it to the flour and butter with the egg and mix to a smooth dough. Cover and leave in a warm place for about 1 hour until doubled in size.

Turn out on to a floured surface and knead well. Roll out one-third of the dough and use to line the base of a greased 23 cm/9 in loose-bottomed cake tin (pan). Spread the custard filling over the dough.

Roll out the remaining dough to a rectangle about 5 mm/¼ in thick. Cream together the remaining butter or margarine and the icing sugar, then mix in the currants. Spread over the dough, leaving a gap around the edges, then roll up the dough from the shorter side. Cut into slices and arrange on top of the custard filling. Cover and leave in a warm place to rise for about 1 hour. Bake in a preheated oven at 230°C/450°F/gas mark 8 for 25–30 minutes until well risen and golden on top.

Danish Cardamom Cake

Makes one 900 g/2 lb cake

225 g/8 oz/1 cup butter or margarine, softened

225 g/8 oz/1 cup caster (superfine) sugar

3 eggs

350 g/12 oz/3 cups plain (all-purpose) flour

10 ml/2 tsp baking powder

10 cardamom seeds, ground

150 ml/¼ pt/2/3 cup milk

45 ml/3 tbsp raisins

45 ml/3 tbsp chopped mixed (candied) peel

Cream together the butter or margarine and sugar until light and fluffy. Add the eggs, a little at a time, beating well after each addition. Fold in the flour, baking powder and cardamom. Gradually stir in the milk, raisins and mixed peel. Spoon into a greased and lined 900 g/2 lb loaf tin (pan) and bake in a preheated oven at 190°C/375°F/ gas mark 5 for 50 minutes until a skewer inserted in the centre comes out clean.

Gâteau Pithiviers

Makes one 25 cm/10 in cake

100 g/4 oz/½ cup butter or margarine, softened

100 g/4 oz/½ cup caster (superfine) sugar

1 egg

1 egg yolk

100 g/4 oz/1 cup ground almonds

30 ml/2 tbsp rum

400 g/14 oz Puff Pastry

For the glaze:

1 egg, beaten

30 ml/2 tbsp icing (confectioners') sugar

Beat together the butter or margarine and sugar until light and fluffy. Beat in the egg and egg yolk, then beat in the almonds and rum. Roll out half the pastry (paste) on a lightly floured surface and cut into a 23 cm/9 in circle. Place on a dampened baking (cookie) sheet and spread the filling over the pastry to within 1 cm/½ in of the edge. Roll out the remaining pastry and cut into a 25 cm/ 10 in circle. Cut a 1 cm/½ in ring off the edge of this circle. Brush the edge of the pastry base with water and press the ring round the edge, gently pushing it to fit. Brush with water and press the second circle over the top, sealing the edges. Seal and flute the edges. Brush the top with beaten egg, then mark a pattern of radial cuts on the top with the blade of a knife. Bake in a preheated oven at 220°C/425°F/gas mark 7 for 30 minutes until risen and golden brown. Sift the icing sugar over the top and return to the oven for a further 5 minutes until shiny. Serve warm or cold.

Galette des Rois

Makes one 18 cm/7 in cake

250 g/9 oz/2¼ cups plain (all-purpose) flour

5 ml/1 tsp salt

200 g/7 oz/scant 1 cup unsalted (sweet) butter, diced

175 ml/6 fl oz/¾ cup water

1 egg

1 egg white

Place the flour and salt in a bowl and make a well in the centre. Add 75 g/ 3 oz/1/3 cup of the butter, the water and whole egg and mix to a soft dough. Cover and leave to stand for 30 minutes.

Roll out the dough into a long rectangle on a lightly floured surface. Dot two-thirds of the dough with one-third of the remaining butter. Fold the uncovered pastry up over the butter, then fold the remaining pastry over the top. Seal the edges and chill for 10 minutes. Roll out the dough again and repeat with half the remaining butter. Chill, roll out and add the remaining butter, then chill for a final 10 minutes.

Roll out the dough into a 2.5 cm/1 in thick circle about 18 cm/7 in in diameter. Place on a greased baking (cookie) sheet, brush with egg white and leave to stand for 15 minutes. Bake in a preheated oven at 180°C/350°F/gas mark 4 for 15 minutes until well risen and golden brown.

Crème Caramel

Makes one 15 cm/6 in cake

For the caramel:

100 g/4 oz/½ cup caster (superfine) sugar

150 ml/¼ pt/2/3 cup water

For the custard:

600 ml/1 pt/2½ cups milk

4 eggs, lightly beaten

15 ml/1 tbsp caster (superfine) sugar

1 orange

To make the caramel, place the sugar and water in a small pan and dissolve over a low heat. Bring to the boil, then boil without stirring for about 10 minutes until the syrup turns a rich golden brown. Pour into a 15 cm/6 in soufflé dish and tilt the dish so the caramel flows over the base.

To make the custard, warm the milk, then pour it on to the eggs and sugar and whisk thoroughly. Pour into the dish. Stand the dish in a baking tin (pan) with hot water to half-way up the sides of the dish. Bake in a preheated oven at 170°C/325°F/gas mark 3 for 1 hour until set. Leave until cold before turning out on to a serving plate. Peel the orange and slice horizontally, then cut each slice in half. Arange around the caramel to decorate.

Gugelhopf

Makes one 20 cm/8 in cake

25 g/1 oz fresh yeast or 40 ml/ 2½ tbsp dried yeast

120 ml/4 fl oz/½ cup warm milk

100 g/4 oz/2/3 cup raisins

15 ml/1 tbsp rum

450 g/1 lb/4 cups strong plain (bread) flour

5 ml/1 tsp salt

A pinch of grated nutmeg

100 g/4 oz/½ cup caster (superfine) sugar

Grated rind of 1 lemon

175 g/6 oz/¾ cup butter or margarine, softened

3 eggs

100 g/4 oz/1 cup blanched almonds

Icing (confectioners') sugar for dusting

Blend the yeast with a little of the warm milk and leave in a warm place for 20 minutes until frothy. Place the raisins in a bowl, sprinkle with the rum and leave to soak. Place the flour, salt and nutmeg in a bowl and stir in the sugar and lemon rind. Make a well in the centre, pour in the yeast mixture, the remaining milk, the butter or margarine and the eggs and work together to make a dough. Place in an oiled bowl, cover with oiled clingfilm (plastic wrap) and leave in a warm place for 1 hour until doubled in size. Generously butter a 20 cm/8 in gugelhopf tin (fluted tube pan) and place the almonds around the base. Knead the raisins and rum into the risen dough and mix well. Spoon the mixture into the tin, cover and leave in a warm place for 40 minutes until the dough has almost doubled in volume and reached to the top of the tin. Bake in a preheated oven at 200°C/400°F/gas mark 6 for 45 minutes until a skewer inserted in the centre comes out clean. Cover with a double layer of greaseproof (waxed) paper towards the end of the cooking if the cake is over-browning. Turn out and leave to cool, then dust with icing sugar.

Luxury Chocolate Gugelhopf

Makes one 20 cm/8 in cake

25 g/1 oz fresh yeast or 40 ml/2½ tbsp dried yeast

120 ml/4 fl oz/½ cup warm milk

50 g/2 oz/1/3 cup raisins

50 g/2 oz/1/3 cup currants

25 g/1 oz/3 tbsp chopped mixed (candied) peel

15 ml/1 tbsp rum

450 g/1 lb/4 cups strong plain (bread) flour

5 ml/1 tsp salt

5 ml/1 tsp ground allspice

A pinch of ground ginger

100 g/4 oz/½ cup caster (superfine) sugar

Grated rind of 1 lemon

175 g/6 oz/¾ cup butter or margarine, softened

3 eggs

For the topping:
60 ml/4 tbsp apricot jam (conserve), sieved (strained)

30 ml/2 tbsp water

100 g/4 oz/1 cup plain (semi-sweet) chocolate

50 g/2 oz/½ cup flaked (slivered) almonds, toasted

Blend the yeast with a little of the warm milk and leave in a warm place for 20 minutes until frothy. Place the raisins, currants and mixed peel in a bowl, sprinkle with the rum and leave to soak. Place the flour, salt and spices in a bowl and stir in the sugar and lemon rind. Make a well in the centre, pour in the yeast mixture, the remaining milk and the eggs and work together to make a dough. Place in an oiled bowl, cover with oiled clingfilm (plastic wrap) and leave in a warm place for 1 hour until doubled in size. Knead the fruit and rum into the risen dough and mix well. Spoon the mixture into a well-buttered 20 cm/8 in gugelhopf tin (fluted tube pan), cover and leave in a warm place for 40 minutes until the dough has almost doubled in volume and reached to the top of the tin. Bake in a preheated oven at 200°C/400°F/gas mark 6 for 45 minutes until a skewer inserted in the centre comes out clean. Cover with a double layer of greaseproof (waxed) paper towards the end of the cooking if the cake is becoming too brown. Turn out and leave to cool.

Heat the jam with the water, stirring until well blended. Brush over the cake. Melt the chocolate in a heatproof bowl set over a pan of gently simmering water. Spread over the cake and press the flaked almonds around the base before the chocolate sets.

Stollen

Makes three 350 g/12 oz cakes

15 g/½ oz fresh yeast or 20 ml/4 tsp dried yeast

15 ml/1 tbsp caster (superfine) sugar

120 ml/4 fl oz/½ cup warm water

25 g/1 oz/¼ cup strong plain (bread) flour

For the fruit dough:

450 g/1 lb/4 cups strong plain (bread) flour

5 ml/1 tsp salt

75 g/3 oz/1/3 cup demerara sugar

1 egg, lightly beaten

225 g/8 oz/11/3 cups raisins

30 ml/2 tbsp rum

50 g/2 oz/1/3 cup chopped mixed (candied) peel

50 g/2 oz/½ cup ground almonds

5 ml/1 tsp ground cinnamon

100 g/4 oz/½ cup butter or margarine, melted

175 g/6 oz Almond Paste

For the glaze:

1 egg, lightly beaten

75 g/3 oz/1/3 cup caster (superfine) sugar

90 ml/6 tbsp water

50 g/2 oz/½ cup flaked (slivered) almonds

Icing (confectioners') sugar for dusting

To make the yeast mixture, mix the yeast and sugar to a paste with the warm water and flour. Leave in a warm place for 20 minutes until frothy.

To make the fruit dough, place the flour and salt in a bowl, stir in the sugar and make a well in the centre. Add the egg with the yeast mixture and mix to a smooth dough. Add the raisins, rum, mixed peel, ground almonds and cinnamon and knead until well blended and smooth. Place in an oiled bowl, cover with oiled clingfilm (plastic wrap) and leave in a warm place for 30 minutes.

Divide the dough into thirds and roll out into rectangles about 1 cm/½ in thick. Brush the butter over the top. Divide the almond paste into thirds and roll into sausage shapes. Place one in the centre of each rectangle and fold the pastry over the top. Turn over with the seam underneath and place on a greased baking (cookie) sheet. Brush with egg, cover with oiled clingfilm (plastic wrap) and leave in a warm place for 40 minutes until doubled in size.

Bake in a preheated oven at 220°C/ 425°F/gas mark 7 for 30 minutes until golden brown.

Meanwhile, boil the sugar with the water for 3 minutes until you have a thick syrup. Brush the top of each stollen with the syrup and sprinkle with flaked almonds and icing sugar.

Almond Stollen

Makes two 450 g/1 lb loaves

15 g/½ oz fresh yeast or 20 ml/ 4 tsp dried yeast

50 g/2 oz/¼ cup caster (superfine) sugar

300 ml/½ pt/1¼ cups warm milk

1 egg

Grated rind of 1 lemon

A pinch of grated nutmeg

450 g/1 lb/4 cups plain (all-purpose) flour

A pinch of salt

100 g/4 oz/2/3 cup chopped mixed (candied) peel

175 g/6 oz/1½ cups almonds, chopped

50 g/2 oz/¼ cup butter or margarine, melted

75 g/3 oz/½ cup icing (confectioners') sugar, sifted, for dusting

Blend the yeast with 5 ml/1 tsp of the sugar and a little of the warm milk and leave in a warm place for 20 minutes until frothy. Beat the egg with the remaining sugar, the lemon rind and nutmeg, then beat into the yeast mixture with the flour, salt and remaining warm milk and mix to a soft dough. Place in an oiled bowl, cover with oiled clingfilm (plastic wrap) and leave in a warm place for 30 minutes.

Knead in the mixed peel and almonds, cover again and leave in a warm place for 30 minutes until doubled in size.

Divide the dough into halves. Roll one half into a 30 cm/12 in sausage shape. Press the rolling pin into the centre to make a dip, then fold over one side lengthways and press down gently. Repeat with the other half. Place both on a greased and lined baking (cookie) sheet, cover with oiled clingfilm (plastic wrap) and leave in a warm place for 25 minutes until doubled in size. Bake in a preheated oven at 200°C/400°F/gas mark 6 for 1 hour until golden and a skewer inserted in the centre comes out clean. Brush the warm loaves generously with the melted butter and sprinkle with the icing sugar.

Pistachio Nut Stollen

Makes two 450 g/1 lb loaves

15 g/½ oz fresh yeast or 20 ml/ 4 tsp dried yeast

50 g/2 oz/¼ cup caster (superfine) sugar

300 ml/½ pt/1¼ cups warm milk

1 egg

Grated rind of 1 lemon

A pinch of grated nutmeg

450 g/1 lb/4 cups plain (all-purpose) flour

A pinch of salt

100 g/4 oz/2/3 cup chopped mixed (candied) peel

100 g/4 oz/1 cup pistachio nuts, chopped

100 g/4 oz Almond Paste

15 ml/1 tbsp maraschino liqueur

50 g/2 oz/1/3 cup icing (confectioners') sugar, sifted

For the topping:
50 g/2 oz/¼ cup butter or margarine, melted

75 g/3 oz/½ cup icing (confectioners') sugar, sifted, for dusting

Blend the yeast with 5 ml/1 tsp of the sugar and a little of the warm milk and leave in a warm place for 20 minutes until frothy. Beat the egg with the remaining sugar, the lemon rind and nutmeg, then beat into the yeast mixture with the flour, salt and remaining warm milk and mix to a soft dough. Place in an oiled bowl, cover with oiled clingfilm (plastic wrap) and leave in a warm place for 30 minutes.

Knead in the mixed peel and pistachio nuts, cover again and leave in a warm place for 30 minutes until doubled in size. Work the almond paste, liqueur and icing sugar to a paste, roll out to 1 cm/½ in thick and cut into cubes. Work into the dough so that the cubes remain whole.

Divide the dough into halves. Roll one half into a 30 cm/12 in sausage shape. Press the rolling pin into the centre to make a dip, then fold over one side lengthways and press down gently. Repeat with the second half. Place both on a greased and lined baking (cookie) sheet, cover with oiled clingfilm (plastic wrap) and leave in a warm place for 25 minutes until doubled in size. Bake in a preheated oven at 200°C/400°F/gas mark 6 for 1 hour until golden and a skewer inserted in the centre comes out clean. Brush the warm loaves generously with the melted butter and dust with the icing sugar.

Baklava

Makes 24

450 g/1 lb/2 cups caster (superfine) sugar

300 ml/½ pt/1¼ cups water

5 ml/1 tsp lemon juice

30 ml/2 tbsp rose water

350 g/12 oz/1½ cups unsalted (sweet) butter, melted

450 g/1 lb filo pastry (paste)

675 g/1½ lb/6 cups almonds, finely chopped

To make the syrup, dissolve the sugar in the water over a low heat, stirring occasionally. Add the lemon juice and bring to the boil. Boil for 10 minutes until syrupy, then add the rose water and leave to cool, then chill.

Brush a large roasting tin with melted butter. Layer half the sheets of filo in the tin, brushing each one with butter. Fold up the edges to hold in the filling. Spread the almonds over the top. Continue to layer the remaining pastry, brushing each sheet with melted butter. Brush the top generously with butter. Cut the pastry into lozenge shapes about 5 cm/2 in wide. Bake in a preheated oven at 180°C/350°F/ gas mark 4 for 25 minutes until crisp and golden. Pour the cool syrup over the top, then leave to cool.

Hungarian Stressel Whirls

Makes 16

25 g/1 oz fresh yeast or 40 ml/ 2½ tbsp dried yeast

15 ml/1 tbsp soft brown sugar

300 ml/½ pt/1¼ cups warm water

15 ml/1 tbsp butter or margarine

450 g/1 lb/4 cups wholemeal (wholewheat) flour

15 ml/1 tbsp milk powder (non-fat dry milk)

5 ml/1 tsp ground mixed (apple-pie) spice

2.5 ml/½ tsp salt

1 egg

175 g/6 oz/1 cup currants

100 g/4 oz/2/3 cup sultanas (golden raisins)

50 g/2 oz/1/3 cup raisins

50 g/2 oz/1/3 cup chopped mixed (candied) peel

For the topping:

75 g/3 oz/¾ cup wholemeal (wholewheat) flour

50 g/2 oz/¼ cup butter or margarine, melted

75 g/3 oz/1/3 cup soft brown sugar

25 g/1 oz/¼ cup sesame seeds

For the filling:

50 g/2 oz/¼ cup soft brown sugar

50 g/2 oz/¼ cup butter or margarine, softened

50 g/2 oz/½ cup ground almonds

2.5 ml/½ tsp grated nutmeg

25 g/2 oz/1/3 cup stoned (pitted) prunes, chopped

1 egg, beaten

Mix together the yeast and sugar with a little of the warm water and leave in a warm place for 10 minutes until frothy. Rub the butter or margarine into the flour, then stir in the milk powder, mixed spice and salt and make a well in the centre. Stir in the egg, the yeast mixture and the remaining warm water and mix to a dough. Knead until smooth and elastic. Knead in the currants, sultanas, raisins and mixed peel. Place in an oiled bowl, cover with oiled clingfilm (plastic wrap) and leave in warm place for 1 hour.

Mix together the topping ingredients until crumbly. To make the filling, cream together the butter or margarine and sugar, then mix in the almonds and nutmeg. Roll out the dough to a large rectangle about 1 cm/½ in thick. Spread with the filling and sprinkle with the prunes. Roll up like a Swiss (jelly) roll, brushing the edges with egg to seal together. Cut into 2.5 cm/1 in slices and arrange in a greased, shallow baking tin (pan). Brush with egg and sprinkle with the topping mixture. Cover and leave in a warm place to rise for 30 minutes. Bake in a preheated oven at 220°C/425°F/gas mark 7 for 30 minutes.

Panforte

Makes one 23 cm/9 in cake

175 g/6 oz/¾ cup granulated sugar

175 g/6 oz/½ cup clear honey

100 g/4 oz/2/3 cup dried figs, chopped

100 g/4 oz/2/3 cup chopped mixed (candied) peel

50 g/2 oz/¼ cup glacé cherries (candied), chopped

50 g/2 oz/¼ cup glacé (candied) pineapple, chopped

175 g/6 oz/1½ cups blanched almonds, coarsely chopped

100 g/4 oz/1 cup walnuts, coarsely chopped

100 g/4 oz/1 cup hazelnuts, coarsely chopped

50 g/2 oz/½ cup plain (all-purpose) flour

25 g/1 oz/¼ cup cocoa (unsweetened chocolate) powder

5 ml/1 tsp ground cinnamon

A pinch of grated nutmeg

15 ml/1 tbsp icing (confectioners') sugar, sifted

Dissolve the granulated sugar in the honey in a pan over a low heat. Bring to the boil and boil for 2 minutes until you have a thick syrup. Mix together the fruit and nuts and stir in the flour, cocoa and spices. Stir in the syrup. Spoon the mixture into a greased 23 cm/9 in sandwich tin (pan) lined with rice paper. Bake in a preheated oven at 180°C/350°F/ gas mark 4 for 45 minutes. Leave to cool in the tin for 15 minutes, then turn out on to a wire rack to cool. Sprinkle with the icing sugar before serving.

Pasta Ribbon Cake

Makes one 23 cm/9 in cake

300 g/11 oz/2¾ cups plain (all-purpose) flour

50 g/2 oz/¼ cup butter or margarine, melted

3 eggs, beaten

A pinch of salt

225 g/8 oz/2 cups almonds, chopped

200 g/7 oz/scant 1 cup caster (superfine) sugar

Grated rind and juice of 1 lemon

90 ml/6 tbsp kirsch

Place the flour in a bowl and make a well in the centre. Stir in the butter, eggs and salt and mix to a soft dough. Roll out thinly and cut into narrow ribbons. Mix together the almonds, sugar and lemon rind. Grease a 23 cm/9 in cake tin (pan) and sprinkle with flour. Arrange a layer of the pasta ribbons in the base of the tin, sprinkle with a little of the almond mixture and drizzle with a little of the kirsch. Continue layering, ending with a layer of pasta. Cover with buttered greaseproof (waxed) paper and bake at 180°C/ 350°F/gas mark 4 for 1 hour. Turn out carefully and serve warm or cold.

Italian Rice Cake with Grand Marnier

Makes one 20 cm/8 in cake

1.5 litres/2½ pts/6 cups milk

A pinch of salt

350 g/12 oz/1½ cups arborio or other medium-grain rice

Grated rind of 1 lemon

60 ml/4 tbsp caster (superfine) sugar

3 eggs

25 g/1 oz/2 tbsp butter or margarine

1 egg yolk

30 ml/2 tbsp chopped mixed (candied) peel

225 g/8 oz/2 cups slivered (flaked) almonds, toasted

45 ml/3 tbsp Grand Marnier

30 ml/2 tbsp dried breadcrumbs

Bring the milk and salt to the boil in a heavy pan, add the rice and lemon rind, cover and simmer for 18 minutes, stirring occasionally. Remove from the heat and stir in the sugar, eggs and butter or margarine and leave until lukewarm. Beat in the egg yolk, mixed peel, nuts and Grand Marnier. Grease a 20 cm/8 in cake tin (pan) and sprinkle with the breadcrumbs. Spoon the mixture into the tin and bake in a preheated oven at 150°C/ 300°F/gas mark 2 for 45 minutes until a skewer inserted in the centre comes out clean. Leave to cool in the tin, then turn out and serve warm.

Sicilian Sponge Cake

Makes one 23 x 9 cm/7 x 3½ in cake

450 g/1 lb Madeira Cake

For the filling:

450 g/1 lb/2 cups Ricotta cheese

50 g/2 oz/¼ cup caster (superfine) sugar

30 ml/2 tbsp double (heavy) cream

30 ml/2 tbsp chopped mixed (candied) peel

15 ml/1 tbsp chopped almonds

30 ml/2 tbsp orange-flavoured liqueur

50 g/2 oz /½ cup plain (semi-sweet) chocolate, grated

For the icing (frosting):

350 g/12 oz/3 cups plain (semi-sweet) chocolate

175 ml/6 fl oz/¾ cup strong black coffee

225 g/8 oz/1 cup unsalted (sweet) butter or margarine

Cut the cake lengthways into 1 cm/½ in slices. To make the filling, press the Ricotta through a sieve (strainer), then beat until smooth. Beat in the sugar, cream, mixed peel, almonds, liqueur and chocolate. Arrange layers of cake and Ricotta mixture in a foil-lined 450 g/1 lb loaf tin (pan), finishing with a layer of cake. Fold the foil over the top and chill for 3 hours until firm.

To make the icing, melt the chocolate and coffee in a heatproof bowl set over a pan of gently simmering water. Beat in the butter or margarine and continue to beat until the mixture is smooth. Leave to cool until thick.

Remove the cake from the foil and place on a serving plate. Pipe or spread the icing over the top and sides of the cake and mark into patterns with a fork, if liked. Chill until firm.

Italian Ricotta Cake

Makes one 25 cm/10 in cake

For the sauce:

225 g/8 oz raspberries

250 ml/8 fl oz/1 cup water

50 g/2 oz/¼ cup caster (superfine) sugar

30 ml/2 tbsp cornflour (cornstarch)

For the filling:

450 g/1 lb/ 2 cups Ricotta cheese

225 g/8 oz/1 cup cream cheese

75 g/3 oz/1/3 cup caster (superfine) sugar

5 ml/1 tsp vanilla essence (extract)

Grated rind of 1 lemon

Grated rind of 1 orange

One 25 cm/10 in Angel Food Cake

To make the sauce, purée the ingredients until smooth, then pour into a small pan and cook over a medium heat, stirring, until the sauce thickens and just comes to the boil. Strain and discard the seeds, if you prefer. Cover and chill.

To make the filling, beat together all the ingredients until well mixed.

Cut the cake horizontally into three layers and sandwich them together with two-thirds of the filling, spreading the remainder on the top. Cover and chill until ready to serve with the sauce poured over the top.

Italian Vermicelli Cake

Makes one 23 cm/9 in cake

225 g/8 oz vermicelli

4 eggs, separated

200 g/7 oz/scant 1 cup caster (superfine) sugar

225 g/8 oz Ricotta cheese

2.5 ml/½ tsp ground cinnamon

2.5 ml/½ tsp ground cloves

A pinch of salt

50 g/2 oz/½ cup plain (all-purpose) flour

50 g/2 oz/1/3 cup raisins

45 ml/3 tbsp clear honey

Single (light) or double (heavy) cream to serve

Bring a large pan of water to the boil, add the pasta and boil for 2 minutes. Drain and rinse under cold water. Beat the egg yolks with the sugar until pale and fluffy. Beat in the Ricotta, cinnamon, cloves and salt, then fold in the flour. Stir in the raisins and pasta. Beat the egg whites until they form soft peaks, then fold into the cake mixture. Pour into a greased and lined 23 cm/9 in cake tin (pan) and bake in a preheated oven at 200°C/400°F/gas mark 6 for 1 hour until golden. Heat the honey gently and pour it over the warm cake. Serve warm with cream.

Italian Walnut and Mascarpone Cake

Makes one 23 cm/9 in cake

450 g/1 lb Puff Pastry

175 g/6 oz/¾ cup Mascarpone cheese

50 g/2 oz/¼ cup caster (superfine) sugar

30 ml/2 tbsp apricot jam (conserve)

3 egg yolks

50 g/2 oz/½ cup walnuts, chopped

100 g/4 oz/2/3 cup chopped mixed (candied) peel

Finely grated rind of 1 lemon

Icing (confectioners') sugar, sifted, for dusting

Roll out the pastry and use half to line a greased 23 cm/9 in flan tin (pan). Beat the Mascarpone with the sugar, jam and 2 egg yolks. Reserve 15 ml/1 tbsp of the nuts for decoration, then fold the remainder into the mixture with the mixed peel and lemon rind. Spoon into the pastry case (pie shell). Cover the filling with the remaining pastry (paste), then dampen and seal the edges together. Beat the remaining egg yolk and brush over the top. Bake in a preheated oven at 200°C/400°F/gas mark 6 for 35 minutes until risen and golden brown. Sprinkle with the reserved walnuts and dust with icing sugar.

Dutch Apple Cake

Serves 8

150 g/5 oz/2/3 cup butter or margarine

225 g/8 oz/2 cups plain (all-purpose) flour

5 ml/1 tsp baking powder

2 eggs, separated

10 ml/2 tsp lemon juice

900 g/2 lb unpeeled cooking (tart) apples, cored and sliced

175 g/6 oz/1 cup ready-to-eat dried apricots, quartered

100 g/4 oz/2/3 cup raisins

30 ml/2 tbsp water

5 ml/1 tsp ground cinnamon

50 g/2 oz/½ cup ground almonds

Rub the butter or margarine into the flour and baking powder until the mixture resembles breadcrumbs. Add the egg yolks and 5 ml/1 tsp of the lemon juice and mix to a soft dough. Roll out two-thirds of the pastry (paste) and use to line a greased 23 cm/9 in cake tin (pan).

Place the apple slices, apricots and raisins in a pan with the remaining lemon juice and the water. Simmer gently for 5 minutes, then drain. Spoon the fruit into the pastry case. Mix together the cinnamon and ground almonds and sprinkle over the top. Roll out the remaining pastry and make a lid for the cake. Seal the edge with a little water and brush the top with egg white. Bake in a preheated oven at 180°C/350°F/gas mark 4 for about 45 minutes until firm and golden.

Norwegian Plain Cake

Makes one 25 cm/10 in cake

225 g/8 oz/1 cup butter or margarine, softened

275 g/10 oz/1¼ cups caster (superfine) sugar

5 eggs

175 g/6 oz/1½ cups plain (all-purpose) flour

7.5 ml/1½ tsp baking powder

A pinch of salt

5 ml/1 tsp almond essence (extract)

Cream the butter or margarine and sugar until well blended. Gradually add the eggs, beating well after each addition. Beat in the flour, baking powder, salt and almond essence until smooth. Spoon into an ungreased 25 cm/10 in cake tin (pan) and bake in a preheated oven at 160°C/320°F/gas mark 3 for 1 hour until firm to the touch. Leave to cool in the tin for 10 minutes before turning out on to a wire rack to finish cooling.

Norwegian Kransekake

Makes one 25 cm/10 in cake

450 g/1 lb/4 cups ground almonds

100 g/4 oz/1 cup ground bitter almonds

450 g/1 lb/22/3 cups icing (confectioners') sugar

3 egg whites

For the icing (frosting):
75 g/3 oz/½ cup icing (confectioners') sugar

½ egg white

2.5 ml/½ tsp lemon juice

Mix together the almonds and icing sugar in a pan. Stir in one egg white, then place the mixture over a low heat until it is lukewarm. Remove from the heat and mix in the remaining egg whites. Spoon the mixture into a piping bag with a 1 cm/½ in fluted nozzle (tip) and pipe a spiral 25 cm/10 in in diameter on a greased baking (cookie) sheet. Continue to pipe into spirals, each one 5 mm/¼ in smaller than the last, until you have a 5 cm/2 in circle. Bake in a preheated oven at 150°C/300°F/gas mark 2 for about 15 minutes until light brown. While they are still warm, place them one on top of the other to make a tower.

Mix together the icing ingredients and pipe zig-zag lines all over the cake through a fine nozzle.

Portuguese Coconut Cakes

Makes 12

4 eggs, separated

450 g/1 lb/2 cups caster (superfine) sugar

450 g/1 lb/4 cups desiccated (shredded) coconut

100 g/4 oz/1 cup rice flour

50 ml/2 fl oz/3½ tbsp rose water

1.5 ml/¼ tsp ground cinnamon

1.5 ml/¼ tsp ground cardamom

A pinch of ground cloves

A pinch of grated nutmeg

25 g/1 oz/¼ cup flaked (slivered) almonds

Beat together the egg yolks and sugar until pale. Stir in the coconut, then fold in the flour. Stir in the rose water and spices. Whisk the egg whites until stiff, then fold into the mixture. Pour into a greased 25 cm/10 in square baking tin (pan) and sprinkle the almonds over the top. Bake in a preheated oven at 180°C/350°F/gas mark 4 for 50 minutes until a skewer inserted in the centre comes out clean. Leave to cool in the tin for 10 minutes, then cut into squares.

Scandinavian Tosca Cake

Makes one 23 cm/9 in cake

2 eggs

150 g/5 oz/2/3 cup soft brown sugar

50 g/2 oz/¼ cup butter or margarine, melted

10 ml/2 tsp grated orange rind

150 g/5 oz/1¼ cups plain (all-purpose) flour

7.5 ml/1½ tsp baking powder

60 ml/4 tbsp double (heavy) cream

For the topping:

50 g/2 oz/¼ cup butter or margarine

50 g/2 oz/¼ cup caster (superfine) sugar

100 g/4 oz/1 cup almonds, chopped

15 ml/1 tbsp double (heavy) cream

30 ml/2 tbsp plain (all-purpose) flour

Whisk together the eggs and sugar until light and fluffy. Stir in the butter or margarine and orange rind, then fold in the flour and baking powder. Stir in the cream. Spoon the mixture into a greased and lined 23 cm/9 in cake tin (pan) and bake in a preheated oven at 180°C/350°C/gas mark 4 for 20 minutes.

To make the topping, heat the ingredients in a pan, stirring until well blended, and bring to boiling point. Pour over the cake. Increase the oven temperature to 200°C/400°F/gas mark 6 and return the cake to the oven for a further 15 minutes until golden brown.

South African Hertzog Cookies

Makes 12

75 g/3 oz/¾ cup plain (all-purpose) flour

15 ml/1 tbsp caster (superfine) sugar

5 ml/1 tsp baking powder

A pinch of salt

40 g/1½ oz/3 tbsp butter or margarine

1 large egg yolk

5 ml/1 tsp milk

For the filling:

30 ml/2 tbsp apricot jam (conserve)

1 large egg white

100 g/4 oz/½ cup caster (superfine) sugar

50 g/2 oz/½ cup desiccated (shredded) coconut

Mix together the flour, sugar, baking powder and salt. Rub in the butter or margarine until the mixture resembles breadcrumbs. Mix in the egg yolk and enough milk to make a soft dough. Knead well. Roll out the dough on a lightly floured surface, cut into circles with a biscuit (cookie) cutter and use to line greased bun tins (patty pans). Place a spoonful of jam in the centre of each one.

To make the filling, beat the egg white until stiff, then beat in the sugar until stiff and glossy. Stir in the coconut. Spoon the filling into the pastry cases (pie shells), making sure it covers the jam. Bake in a preheated oven at 180°C/350°F/gas mark 4 for 20 minutes until golden. Allow to cool in the tins for 5 minutes before turning out on to a wire rack to finish cooling.

Basque Cake

Makes one 25 cm/10 in cake

For the filling:

50 g/2 oz/¼ cup caster (superfine) sugar

25 g/1 oz/¼ cup cornflour (cornstarch)

2 egg yolks

300 ml/½ pt/1¼ cups milk

½ vanilla pod (bean)

A little icing (confectioners') sugar

For the cake:

275 g/10 oz/1¼ cups butter or margarine, softened

175 g/5 oz/¼ cup caster (superfine) sugar

3 eggs

5 ml/1 tsp vanilla essence (extract)

450 g/1 lb/4 cups plain (all-purpose) flour

10 ml/2 tsp baking powder

A pinch of salt

15 ml/1 tbsp brandy

Icing (confectioners') sugar for dusting

To make the filling, beat half the caster sugar with the cornflour, egg yolks and a little of the milk. Bring the remaining milk and sugar to the boil with the vanilla pod, then slowly pour in the sugar and egg mixture, whisking continuously. Bring to the boil and cook for 3 minutes, beating all the time. Pour into a bowl, sprinkle with icing sugar to prevent a skin forming and leave to cool.

To make the cake, cream together the butter or margarine and caster sugar until light and fluffy. Gradually beat in the eggs and vanilla essence alternately with spoonfuls of flour, baking powder and salt, then fold in the remaining flour. Transfer the mixture to a piping bag with a plain 1 cm/½ in nozzle (tip) and pipe half the mixture in a spiral in the base of a greased and floured 25 cm/10 in cake tin (pan). Pipe a circle on top round the edge to form a lip to contain the filling. Discard the vanilla pod from the filling, stir in the brandy and whisk until smooth, then spoon over the cake mixture. Pipe the remaining cake mixture in a spiral over the top. Bake in a preheated oven at 190°C/375°F/gas mark 5 for 50 minutes until golden brown and firm to the touch. Leave to cool, then dust with icing sugar.

Almond and Cream Cheese Prism

Makes one 23 cm/9 in cake

200 g/7 oz/1¾ cups butter or margarine, softened

100 g/4 oz/½ cup caster (superfine) sugar

1 egg

200 g/7 oz/scant 1 cup cream cheese

5 ml/1 tsp lemon juice

2.5 ml/½ tsp ground cinnamon

75 ml/5 tbsp brandy

90 ml/6 tbsp milk

30 Nice biscuits (cookies)

For the icing (frosting):

60 ml/4 tbsp caster sugar

30 ml/2 tbsp cocoa (unsweetened chocolate) powder

100 g/4 oz/1 cup plain (semi-sweet) chocolate

60 ml/4 tbsp water

50 g/2 oz/¼ cup butter or margarine

100 g/4 oz/1 cup flaked (slivered) almonds

Cream together the butter or margarine and sugar until light and fluffy. Beat in the egg, cream cheese, lemon juice and cinnamon. Lay a large sheet of foil on a work surface. Mix the brandy and milk. Dip 10 biscuits in the brandy mixture and arrange on the foil in a rectangle two biscuits high by five biscuits long. Spread the cheese mixture over the biscuits. Dip the remaining biscuits in the brandy and milk and place on top of the mixture to make a long triangular shape. Fold in the foil and chill overnight.

To make the icing, bring the sugar, cocoa, chocolate and water to the boil in a small pan and boil for 3 minutes. Remove from the heat and beat in the butter. Leave to cool slightly. Remove the foil from the cake and spread the chocolate mixture over the top While still warm press on the almonds. Chill until set.

Black Forest Gâteau

Makes one 18 cm/7 in cake

175 g/6 oz/¾ cup butter or margarine, softened

175 g/6 oz/¾ cup caster (superfine) sugar

3 eggs, lightly beaten

150 g/5 oz/1¼ cups self-raising (self-rising) flour

25 g/1 oz/¼ cup cocoa (unsweetened chocolate) powder

10 ml/2 tsp baking powder

90 ml/6 tbsp cherry jam (conserve)

100 g/4 oz/1 cup plain (semi-sweet) chocolate, finely grated

400 g/14 oz/1 large can black cherries, drained and juice reserved

150 ml/¼ pt/2/3 cup double (heavy) cream, whipped

10 ml/2 tsp arrowroot

Cream together the butter or margarine and sugar until light and fluffy. Gradually beat in the eggs, then work in the flour, cocoa and baking powder. Divide the mixture between two greased and lined 18 cm/7 in sandwich tins (pans) and bake in a preheated oven at 180°C/ 350°F/gas mark 4 for 25 minutes until firm to the touch. Leave to cool.

Sandwich the cakes together with some of the jam and spread the remainder over the sides of the cake. Press the grated chocolate over the sides of the cake. Arrange the cherries attractively over the top. Pipe the cream around the top edge of the cake. Warm the arrowroot with a little of the cherry juice and brush over the fruit to glaze.

Chocolate and Almond Gâteau

Makes one 23 cm/9 in cake

100 g/4 oz/1 cup plain (semi-sweet) chocolate

100 g/4 oz/½ cup butter or margarine, softened

150 g/5 oz/2/3 cup caster (superfine) sugar

3 eggs, separated

50 g/2 oz/½ cup ground almonds

100 g/4 oz/1 cup plain (all-purpose) flour

For the filling:

225 g/8 oz/2 cups plain (semi-sweet) chocolate

300 ml/½ pt/1¼ cups double (heavy) cream

75 g/3 oz/¼ cup raspberry jam (conserve)

Melt the chocolate in a heatproof bowl set over a pan of gently simmering water. Cream together the butter or margarine and sugar, then stir in the chocolate and the egg yolks. Fold in the ground almonds and flour. Whisk the egg whites until stiff, then fold them into the mixture. Spoon into a greased and lined 23 cm/9 in cake tin (pan) and bake in a preheated oven at 180°C/350°F/gas mark 4 for 40 minutes until firm to the touch. Leave to cool, then slice the cake in half horizontally.

To make the filling, melt the chocolate and cream in a heatproof bowl set over a pan of gently simmering water. Stir until smooth, then leave to cool, stirring occasionally. Sandwich the cakes together with the jam and half the chocolate cream, then spread the remaining cream over the top and sides of the cake and leave to set.

Chocolate Cheesecake Gâteau

Makes one 23 cm/9 in cake

For the base:

25 g/1 oz/2 tbsp caster (superfine) sugar

175 g/6 oz/1½ cups digestive biscuit (Graham cracker) crumbs

75 g/3 oz/1/3 cup butter or margarine, melted

For the filling:

100 g/4 oz/1 cup plain (semi-sweet) chocolate

300 g/10 oz/1¼ cups cream cheese

3 eggs, separated

45 ml/3 tbsp cocoa (unsweetened chocolate) powder

25 g/1 oz/¼ cup plain (all-purpose) flour

50g /2 oz/¼ cup soft brown sugar

150 ml/¼ pt/2/3 cup soured (dairy sour) cream

50 g/2 oz/¼ cup caster (superfine) sugar For decoration:

100 g/4 oz/1 cup plain (semi-sweet) chocolate

25 g/1 oz/2 tbsp butter or margarine

120 ml/4 fl oz/½ cup double (heavy) cream

6 glacé (candied) cherries

To make the base, stir the sugar and biscuit crumbs into the melted butter and press into the base and sides of a greased 23 cm/9 in springform cake tin (pan).

To make the filling, melt the chocolate in a heatproof bowl set over a pan of gently simmering water. Leave to cool slightly. Beat the cheese with the egg yolks, cocoa, flour, brown sugar and soured cream, then blend in the melted chocolate. Whisk the egg whites until they form soft peaks, then add the caster sugar and whisk again until stiff and glossy. Fold into the mixture using a metal spoon and spoon over the base, levelling the surface. Bake in a preheated oven at 160°C/325°F/gas mark 3 for 1½ hours. Turn off the oven and leave the cake to cool in the oven with the door ajar. Chill until firm, then remove from the tin.

To decorate, melt the chocolate and butter or margarine in a heatproof bowl set over a pan of gently simmering water. Remove from the heat and leave to cool slightly, then stir in the cream. Swirl the chocolate over the top of the cake in patterns, then decorate with the glacé cherries.

Chocolate Fudge Gâteau

Makes one 20 cm/8 in cake

75 g/3 oz/¾ cup plain (semi-sweet) chocolate, chopped

200 ml/7 fl oz/scant 1 cup milk

225 g/8 oz/1 cup dark brown sugar

75 g/3 oz/1/3 cup butter or margarine, softened

2 eggs, lightly beaten

2.5 ml/½ tsp vanilla essence (extract)

150 g/5 oz/1¼ cups plain (all-purpose) flour

25 g/1 oz/¼ cup cocoa (unsweetened chocolate) powder

5 ml/1 tsp bicarbonate of soda (baking soda)

For the icing (frosting):

100 g/4 oz/1 cup plain (semi-sweet) chocolate

100 g/4 oz/½ cup butter or margarine, softened

225 g/8 oz/11/3 cups icing (confectioners') sugar, sifted

Chocolate flakes or curls to decorate

Melt together the chocolate, milk and 75 g/3 oz/1/3 cup of the sugar in a pan, then leave to cool slightly. Cream together the butter and the remaining sugar until light and fluffy. Gradually beat in the eggs and vanilla essence, then stir in the chocolate mixture. Gently fold in the flour, cocoa and bicarbonate of soda. Spoon the mixture into two greased and lined 20 cm/8 in sandwich tins (pans) and bake in a preheated oven at 180°C/350°F/ gas mark 4 for 30 minutes until springy to the touch. Leave to cool in the tins for 3 minutes, then turn out on to a wire rack to finish cooling.

To make the icing, melt the chocolate in a heatproof bowl set over a pan of gently simmering water. Beat together the butter or margarine and sugar until soft, then stir in the melted chocolate. Sandwich the cakes together with one-third of the icing, then spread the rest over the top and sides of the cake. Decorate the top with crumbled flakes or make curls by scraping a sharp knife along the side of a bar of chocolate.

Carob Mint Gâteau

Makes one 20 cm/8 in cake

3 eggs

50 g/2 oz/¼ cup caster (superfine) sugar

75 g/3 oz/1/3 cup self-raising (self-rising) flour

25 g/1 oz/¼ cup carob powder

150 ml/¼ pt/2/3 cup whipping cream

A few drops of peppermint essence (extract)

50 g/2 oz/½ cup chopped mixed nuts

Beat the eggs until pale. Beat in the sugar and continue until the mixture is pale and creamy and trails off the whisk in ribbons. This may take 15–20 minutes. Mix together the flour and carob powder and fold into the egg mixture. Spoon into two greased and lined 20 cm/18 in cake tins (pans) and bake in a preheated oven at 180°C/350°F/gas mark 4 for 15 minutes until springy to the touch. Cool.

Whip the cream to soft peaks, stir in the essence and nuts. Slice each cake in half horizontally and sandwich all the cakes together with the cream.

Iced Coffee Gâteau

Makes one 18 cm/7 in cake

225 g/8 oz/1 cup butter or margarine

100 g/4 oz/½ cup caster (superfine) sugar

2 eggs, lightly beaten

100 g/4 oz/1 cup self-raising (self-rising) flour

A pinch of salt

30 ml/2 tbsp coffee essence (extract)

100 g/4 oz/1 cup flaked (slivered) almonds

225 g/8 oz/11/3 cups icing (confectioners') sugar, sifted

Cream together half the butter or margarine and the caster sugar until light and fluffy. Gradually beat in the eggs, then fold in the flour, salt and 15 ml/ 1 tbsp of the coffee essence. Spoon the mixture into two greased and lined 18 cm/7 in sandwich tins (pans) and bake in a preheated oven at 180°C/350°F/gas mark 4 for 25 minutes until firm to the touch. Leave to cool. Place the almonds in a dry frying pan (skillet) and toast over a medium heat, shaking the pan continuously, until golden.

Beat the remaining butter or margarine until soft, then gradually beat in the icing sugar and the remaining coffee essence until you have a spreading consistency. Sandwich the cakes together with one-third of the icing (frosting). Spread half the remaining icing round the sides of the cake and press the toasted almonds into the icing. Spread the remainder over the top of the cake and mark into patterns with a fork.

Coffee and Walnut Ring Gâteau

Makes one 23 cm/9 in cake

For the cake:

15 ml/1 tbsp instant coffee powder

15 ml/1 tbsp milk

100 g/4 oz/1 cup self-raising (self-rising) flour

5 ml/1 tsp baking powder

100 g/4 oz/½ cup butter or margarine, softened

100 g/4 oz/½ cup caster (superfine) sugar

2 eggs, lightly beaten

For the filling:

45 ml/3 tbsp apricot jam (conserve), sieved (strained)

15 ml/1 tbsp water

10 ml/2 tsp instant coffee powder

30 ml/2 tbsp milk

100 g/4 oz/2/3 cup icing (confectioners') sugar, sifted

50 g/2 oz/¼ cup butter or margarine, softened

50 g/2 oz/½ cup walnuts, chopped

For the icing (frosting):

30 ml/2 tbsp instant coffee powder

90 ml/6 tbsp milk

450 g/1 lb/22/3 cups icing (confectioners') sugar, sifted

50 g/2 oz/¼ cup butter or margarine

A few walnut halves to decorate

To make the cake, dissolve the coffee in the milk, then mix into the remaining cake ingredients and beat until everything is well blended. Spoon into a greased 23 cm/9 in ring mould (tube pan) and bake in a preheated oven at 160°C/325°F/gas mark 3 for 40 minutes until springy to the touch. Leave to cool in the tin for 5 minutes, then turn out on to a wire rack to finish cooling. Cut the cake in half horizontally.

To make the filling, heat the jam and water until well blended, then brush over the cut surfaces of the cake. Dissolve the coffee in the milk, then mix into the icing sugar with the butter or margarine and nuts and beat until you have a spreadable consistency. Sandwich together the two halves of the cake with the filling.

To make the icing, dissolve the coffee in the milk in a heatproof bowl set over a pan of gently simmering water. Add the icing sugar and butter or margarine and beat until smooth. Remove from the heat and leave to cool and thicken to coating consistency, beating occasionally. Spoon the icing over the cake, decorate with walnut halves and leave to set.

Danish Chocolate and Custard Gâteau

Makes one 23 cm/9 in cake

4 eggs, separated

175 g/6 oz/1 cup icing (confectioners') sugar, sifted

Grated rind of ½ lemon

60 g/2½ oz/2/3 cup plain (all-purpose) flour

60 g/2½ oz/2/3 cup potato flour

2.5 ml/½ tsp baking powder

For the filling:

45 ml/3 tbsp caster (superfine) sugar

15 ml/1 tbsp cornflour (cornstarch)

300 ml/½ pt/1¼ cups milk

3 egg yolks, beaten

50 g/2 oz/½ cup chopped mixed nuts

150 ml/¼ pt/2/3 cup double (heavy) cream

For the topping:

100 g/4 oz/1 cup plain (semi-sweet) chocolate

30 ml/2 tbsp double (heavy) cream

25 g/1 oz/¼ cup white chocolate, grated or sliced into curls

Beat the egg yolks into the icing sugar and lemon rind. Stir in the flours and baking powder. Whisk the egg whites until stiff, then fold into the mixture using a metal spoon. Spoon into a greased and lined 23 cm/9 in cake tin (pan) and bake in a preheated oven at 190°C/375°F/gas mark 5 for 20 minutes until golden brown and springy to the touch. Leave to cool in the tin for 5 minutes, then turn out on to a wire rack to finish cooling. Slice the cake horizontally into three layers.

To make the filling, blend the sugar and cornflour to a paste with a little of the milk. Bring the remaining milk just to the boil, then pour on to the cornflour mixture and blend well. Return to the rinsed-out pan and stir continuously over a very gentle heat until the custard thickens. Beat in the egg yolks over a very low heat without allowing the custard to boil. Leave to cool slightly, then stir in the nuts. Whip the cream until stiff, then fold into the custard. Sandwich the layers together with the custard.

To make the topping, melt the chocolate with the cream in a heatproof bowl set over a pan of gently simmering water. Spread over the top of the cake and decorate with grated white chocolate.

Fruit Gâteau

Makes one 20 cm/8 in cake

1 cooking (tart) apple, peeled, cored and chopped

25 g/1 oz/¼ cup dried figs, chopped

25 g/1 oz/¼ cup raisins

75 g/3 oz/1/3 cup butter or margarine, softened

2 eggs

175 g/6 oz/1½ cups wholemeal (wholewheat) flour

5 ml/1 tsp baking powder

30 ml/2 tbsp skimmed milk

15 ml/1 tbsp gelatine

30 ml/2 tbsp water

400 g/14 oz/1 large can chopped pineapple, drained

300 ml/½ pt/1¼ cups fromage frais

150 ml/¼ pt/2/3 cup whipping cream

Mix together the apple, figs, raisins and butter or margarine. Beat in the eggs. Fold in the flour and baking powder and enough of the milk to mix to a soft mixture. Spoon into a greased 20 cm/8 in cake tin (pan) and bake in a preheated oven at 180°C/350°F/gas mark 4 for 30 minutes until firm to the touch. Remove from the tin and cool on a wire rack.

To make the filling, sprinkle the gelatine on the water in a small bowl and leave until spongy. Stand the bowl in a pan of hot water and leave until dissolved. Leave to cool slightly. Stir into the pineapple, fromage frais and cream and chill until set. Cut the cake in half horizontally and sandwich together with the cream.

Fruit Savarin

Makes one 20 cm/8 in cake

15 g/½ oz fresh yeast or 20 ml/4 tsp dried yeast

45 ml/3 tbsp warm milk

100 g/4 oz/1 cup strong plain (bread) flour

A pinch of salt

5 ml/1 tsp sugar

2 eggs, beaten

50 g/2 oz/¼ cup butter or margarine, softened

For the syrup:
225 g/8 oz/1 cup caster (superfine) sugar

300 ml/½ pt/1¼ cups water

45 ml/3 tbsp kirsch

For the filling:
2 bananas

100 g/4 oz strawberries, sliced

100 g/4 oz raspberries

Blend together the yeast and milk, then work in 15 ml/1 tbsp of the flour. Leave to stand until frothy. Add the remaining flour, the salt, sugar, eggs and butter and beat until you have a soft dough. Spoon into a greased and floured 20 cm/8 in savarin or ring mould (tube pan) and leave in a warm place for about 45 minutes until the mixture almost reaches the top of the tin. Bake in a preheated oven for 30 minutes until golden and shrinking away from the sides of the tin. Turn out on to a wire rack over a tray and prick all over with a skewer.

While the savarin is cooking, make the syrup. Dissolve the sugar in the water over a low heat, stirring occasionally. Bring to the boil and simmer without stirring for 5 minutes until syrupy. Stir in the kirsch. Spoon the hot syrup over the savarin until saturated. Leave to cool.

Thinly slice the bananas and mix with the other fruit and the syrup that has dripped into the tray. Place the savarin on a plate and spoon the fruit into the centre just before serving.

Ginger Layer Cake

Makes one 18 cm/7 in cake

100 g/4 oz/1 cup self-raising (self-rising) flour

5 ml/1 tsp baking powder

100 g/4 oz/½ cup butter or margarine, softened

100 g/4 oz/½ cup caster (superfine) sugar

2 eggs

For the filling and decoration:

150 ml/¼ pt/2/3 cup whipping or double (heavy) cream

100 g/4 oz/1/3 cup ginger marmalade

4 ginger biscuits (cookies), crushed

A few pieces of crystallised (candied) ginger

Beat together all the cake ingredients until well blended. Spoon into two greased and lined 18 cm/7 in sandwich tins (pans) and bake in a preheated oven at 160°C/325°F/gas mark 3 for 25 minutes until golden brown and springy to the touch. Leave to cool in the tins for 5 minutes, then turn out on to a wire rack to finish cooling. Cut each cake in half horizontally.

To make the filling, whip the cream until stiff. Spread the base layer of one cake with half the marmalade and place the second layer on top. Spread with half the cream and top with the next layer. Spread that with the remaining marmalade and top with the final layer. Spread the remaining cream on top and decorate with the biscuit crumbs and crystallised ginger.

Grape and Peach Gâteau

Makes one 20 cm/8 in cake

4 eggs

100 g/4 oz/½ cup caster (superfine) sugar

75 g/6 oz/1½ cups plain (all-purpose) flour

A pinch of salt

For the filling and decoration:

100 g/14 oz/1 large can peaches in syrup

450 ml/¾ pt/2 cups double (heavy) cream

50 g/2 oz/¼ cup caster (superfine) sugar

A few drops of vanilla essence (extract)

100 g/4 oz/1 cup hazelnuts, chopped

100 g/4 oz seedless(pitless) grapes

A sprig of fresh mint

Beat together the eggs and sugar until the mixture is thick and pale and trails off the whisk in ribbons. Sift in the flour and salt and fold in gently until combined. Spoon into a greased and lined 20 cm/8 in springform cake tin (pan) and bake in a preheated oven at 180°C/ 350°F/gas mark 4 for 30 minutes until a skewer inserted in the centre comes out clean. Leave to cool in the tin for 5 minutes, then turn out on to a wire rack to finish cooling. Cut the cake in half horizontally.

Drain the peaches and reserve 90 ml/6 tbsp of the syrup. Thinly slice half the peaches and chop the remainder. Whip the cream with the sugar and vanilla essence until thick. Spread half the cream over the bottom layer of the cake, sprinkle with the chopped peaches and replace the top of the cake. Spread the remaining cream round the sides and over the top of the cake. Press the chopped nuts round the sides. Arrange the sliced peaches around the edge of the top of the cake and the grapes in the centre. Decorate with a sprig of mint.

Lemon Gâteau

Makes one 18 cm/7 in cake

For the cake:

100 g/4 oz/½ cup butter or margarine, softened

100 g/4 oz/½ cup caster (superfine) sugar

2 eggs, lightly beaten

100 g/4 oz/1 cup self-raising (self-rising) flour

A pinch of salt

Grated rind and juice of 1 lemon

For the icing (frosting):

100 g/4 oz/½ cup butter or margarine, softened

225 g/8 oz/11/3 cups icing (confectioners') sugar, sifted

100 g/4 oz/1/3 cup lemon curd

Icing flowers for decoration

To make the cake, cream together the butter or margarine and sugar until light and fluffy. Gradually beat in the eggs, then fold in the flour, salt and lemon rind. Spoon the mixture into two greased and lined 18 cm/7 in sandwich tins (pans) and bake in a preheated oven at 180°C/350°F/gas mark 4 for 25 minutes until firm to the touch. Leave to cool.

To make the icing, beat the butter or margarine until soft, then beat in the icing sugar and lemon juice to make a spreadable consistency. Sandwich the cakes together with the lemon curd and spread three-quarters of the icing over the top and sides of the cake, marking into patterns with a fork. Place the rest of the icing in a piping bag with a star nozzle (tip) and pipe rosettes round the top of the cake. Decorate with icing flowers.

Marron Gâteau

Makes one 25 cm/10 in cake

425 g/15 oz/1 large can chestnut purée

6 eggs, separated

5 ml/1 tsp vanilla essence (extract)

5 ml/1 tsp ground cinnamon

350 g/12 oz/2 cups icing (confectioners') sugar, sifted

100 g/4 oz/1 cup plain (all-purpose) flour

5 ml/1 tsp powdered gelatine

30 ml/2 tbsp water

15 ml/1 tbsp rum

300 ml/½ pt/1¼ cups double (heavy) cream

90 ml/6 tbsp apricot jam (conserve), sieved (strained)

30 ml/2 tbsp water

450 g/1 lb/4 cups plain (semi-sweet) chocolate, broken into pieces

100 g/4 oz Almond Paste

30 ml/2 tbsp chopped pistachio nuts

Sieve the chestnut purée and stir until smooth, then divide in half. Mix one half with the egg yolks, vanilla essence, cinnamon and 50 g/2 oz/1/3 cup of the icing sugar. Whisk the egg whites until stiff, then gradually whisk in 175 g/6 oz/ 1 cup of the icing sugar until the mixture forms stiff peaks. Fold into the egg yolk and chestnut mixture. Fold in the flour and spoon into a greased and lined 25 cm/10 in cake tin (pan). Bake in a preheated oven at 180°C/350°F/gas mark 4 for 45 minutes until springy to the touch. Leave to cool, then cover and leave overnight.

Sprinkle the gelatine over the water in a bowl and leave until spongy. Stand the bowl in a pan of hot water and leave until dissolved. Leave to cool slightly. Mix the remaining chestnut purée with the remaining icing sugar and the rum. Whip the cream until stiff, then fold into the purée with the dissolved gelatine. Cut the cake horizontally into three and sandwich together with the chestnut purée. Trim the edges, then chill for 30 minutes.

Boil the jam with the water until well blended, then brush over the top and sides of the cake. Melt the chocolate in a heatproof bowl set over a pan of gently simmering water. Shape the almond paste into 16 chestnut shapes. Dip the base into the melted chocolate, then into the pistachio nuts. Spread the remaining chocolate over the top and sides of the cake and smooth the surface with a palette knife. Arrange the almond-paste chestnuts round the edge while the chocolate is still warm, and mark into 16 slices. Leave to cool and set.

Millefeuille

Makes one 23 cm/9 in cake

225 g/8 oz Puff Pastry

150 ml/¼ pt/2/3 cup double (heavy) or whipping cream

45 ml/3 tbsp raspberry jam (conserve)

Icing (confectioners') sugar, sifted

Roll out the pastry (paste) to about 3 mm/1/8 in thick and cut into three equal rectangles. Place on a dampened baking (cookie) sheet and bake in a preheated oven at 200°C/400°F/gas mark 6 for 10 minutes until golden. Cool on a wire rack. Whip the cream until stiff. Spread the jam over the top of two of the pastry rectangles. Sandwich together the rectangles with the cream, topping with any remaining cream. Serve sprinkled with icing sugar.

Orange Gâteau

Makes one 18 cm/7 in cake

225 g/8 oz/1 cup butter or margarine, softened

100 g/4 oz/½ cup caster (superfine) sugar

2 eggs, lightly beaten

100 g/4 oz/1 cup self-raising (self-rising) flour

A pinch of salt

Grated rind and juice of 1 orange

225 g/8 oz/11/3 cups icing (confectioners') sugar, sifted

Glacé (candied) orange slices to decorate

Cream together half the butter or margarine and the caster sugar until light and fluffy. Gradually beat in the eggs, then fold in the flour, salt and orange rind. Spoon the mixture into two greased and lined 18 cm/7 in sandwich tins (pans) and bake in a preheated oven at 180°C/ 350°F/gas mark 4 for 25 minutes until firm to the touch. Leave to cool.

Beat the remaining butter or margarine until soft, then beat in the icing sugar and orange juice to make a spreadable consistency. Sandwich the cakes together with one-third of the icing (frosting), then spread the remainder over the top and sides of the cake, marking into patterns with a fork. Decorate with glacé orange slices.

Four-tier Orange Marmalade Gâteau

Makes one 23 cm/9 in cake

For the cake:

200 ml/7 fl oz/scant 1 cup water

25 g/1 oz/2 tbsp butter or margarine

4 eggs, lightly beaten

300 g/11 oz/11/3 cups caster (superfine) sugar

5 ml/1 tsp vanilla essence (extract)

300 g/11 oz/2¾ cups plain (all-purpose) flour

10 ml/2 tsp baking powder

A pinch of salt

For the filling:

30 ml/2 tbsp plain (all-purpose) flour

30 ml/2 tbsp cornflour (cornstarch)

15 ml/1 tbsp caster (superfine) sugar

2 eggs, separated

450 ml/¾ pt/2 cups milk

5 ml/1 tsp vanilla essence (extract)

120 ml/4 fl oz/½ cup sweet sherry

175 g/6 oz/½ cup orange marmalade

120 ml/4 fl oz/½ cup double (heavy) cream

100 g/4 oz peanut brittle, crushed

To make the cake, bring the water to the boil with the butter or margarine. Beat together the eggs and sugar until pale and frothy,

99

then continue to beat until the mixture is very light. Beat in the vanilla essence, sprinkle with flour, baking powder and salt and pour in the boiling butter and water mixture. Mix together just until blended. Spoon into two greased and floured 23 cm/9 in sandwich tins (pans) and bake in a preheated oven at 180°C/350°F/gas mark 4 for 25 minutes until golden brown and springy to the touch. Leave to cool in the tins for 3 minutes, then turn out on to a wire rack to finish cooling. Cut each cake in half horizontally.

To make the filling, mix together the flour, cornflour, sugar and egg yolks to a paste with a little of the milk. Bring the remaining milk to the boil in a pan, then pour it into the mixture and whisk until smooth. Return to the rinsed-out pan and bring to the boil over a low heat, stirring continuously until thick. Remove from the heat and stir in the vanilla essence, then leave to cool slightly. Whisk the egg whites until stiff, then fold in.

Sprinkle the sherry over the four cake layers, spread three with marmalade, then spread the custard over the top. Assemble the layers together into a four-tiered sandwich. Whip the cream until stiff and spoon over the top of the cake. Sprinkle with the peanut brittle.

Pecan and Date Gâteau

Makes one 23 cm/9 in cake

For the cake:

250 ml/8 fl oz/1 cup boiling water

450 g/1 lb/2 cups stoned (pitted) dates, finely chopped

2.5 ml/½ tsp bicarbonate of soda (baking soda)

225 g/8 oz/1 cup butter or magarine, softened

225 g/8 oz/1 cup caster (superfine) sugar

3 eggs

100 g/4 oz/1 cup chopped pecan nuts

5 ml/1 tsp vanilla essence (extract)

350 g/12 oz/3 cups plain (all-purpose) flour

10 ml/2 tsp ground cinnamon

5 ml/1 tsp baking powder

For the icing (frosting):

120 ml/4 fl oz/½ cup water

30 ml/2 tbsp cocoa (unsweetened chocolate) powder

10 ml/2 tsp instant coffee powder

100 g/4 oz/½ cup butter or margarine

400 g/14 oz/21/3 cups icing (confectioners') sugar, sifted

50 g/2 oz/½ cup pecan nuts, finely chopped

To make the cake, pour the boiling water over the dates and bicarbonate of soda and leave to stand until cool. Cream together the butter or margarine and caster sugar until light and fluffy. Gradually beat in the eggs, then stir in the nuts, vanilla essence and dates. Fold in the flour, cinnamon and baking powder. Spoon into two greased 23 cm/9 in sandwich tins (pans) and bake in a preheated oven at 180°C/350°F/gas mark 4 for 30 minutes until springy to the touch. Turn out on to a wire rack to cool.

To make the icing, boil the water, cocoa and coffee in a small pan until you have a thick syrup. Leave to cool. Cream together the butter or margarine and the icing sugar until soft, then beat in the syrup. Sandwich the cakes together with one-third of the icing. Spread half the remaining icing round the sides of the cake, then press on the chopped pecans. Spread most of the remaining icing over the top and pipe a few icing rosettes.

Plum and Cinnamon Gâteau

Makes one 23 cm/9 in cake

350 g/12 oz/1½ cups butter or margarine, softened

175 g/6 oz/¾ cup caster (superfine) sugar

3 eggs

150 g/5 oz/1¼ cups self-raising (self-rising) flour

5 ml/1 tsp baking powder

5 ml/1 tsp ground cinnamon

350 g/12 oz/2 cups icing (confectioners') sugar, sifted

5 ml/1 tsp finely grated orange rind

100 g/4 oz/1 cup hazelnuts, coarsely ground

300 g/11 oz/1 medium can plums, drained

Cream together half the butter or margarine and the caster sugar until light and fluffy. Gradually beat in the eggs, then fold in the flour, baking powder and cinnamon. Spoon into a greased and lined 23 cm/9 in square cake tin (pan) and bake in a preheated oven at 180°C/350°F/ gas mark 4 for 40 minutes until a skewer inserted in the centre comes out clean. Remove from the tin and leave to cool.

Beat the remaining butter or margarine until soft, then mix in the icing sugar and grated orange rind. Cut the cake in half horizontally, then sandwich the two halves together with two-thirds of the icing. Spread most of the remaining icing over the top and sides of the cake. Press the nuts round the sides of the cake and arrange the plums attractively on top. Pipe the remaining icing decoratively round the top edge of the cake.

Prune Layer Gâteau

Makes one 25 cm/10 in cake

For the cake:

225 g/8 oz/1 cup butter or margarine

300 g/10 oz/2¼ cups caster (superfine) sugar

3 eggs, separated

450 g/1 lb/4 cups plain (all-purpose) flour

5 ml/1 tsp baking powder

5 ml/1 tsp bicarbonate of soda (baking soda)

5 ml/1 tsp ground cinnamon

5 ml/1 tsp grated nutmeg

2.5 ml/½ tsp ground cloves

A pinch of salt

250 ml/8 fl oz/1 cup single (light) cream

225 g/8 oz/11/3 cups stoned (pitted) cooked prunes, finely chopped

For the filling:

250 ml/8 fl oz/1 cup single (light) cream

100 g/4 oz/½ cup caster (superfine) sugar

3 egg yolks

225 g/8 oz/11/3 cups stoned (pitted)cooked prunes

30 ml/2 tbsp grated orange rind

5 ml/1 tsp vanilla essence (extract)

50 g/2 oz/½ cup chopped mixed nuts

To make the cake, cream together the butter or margarine and sugar. Gradually beat in the egg yolks, then fold in the flour, baking powder, bicarbonate of soda, spices and salt. Fold in the cream and prunes. Whisk the egg whites until stiff, then fold them in to the mixture. Spoon into three greased and floured 25 cm/10 in sandwich tins (pans) and bake in a preheated oven at 180°C/350°F/ gas mark 4 for 25 minutes until well risen and springy to the touch. Leave to cool.

Mix together all the filling ingredients except the nuts until well blended. Place in a pan and cook over a low heat until thickened, stirring continuously. Spread one-third of the filling over the base cake and sprinkle with one-third of the nuts. Place the second cake on top and cover with half the remaining icing and half the remaining nuts. Place the final cake on top and spread the remaining icing and nuts over the top.

Rainbow-stripe Cake

Makes one 18 cm/7 in cake

For the cake:

100 g/4 oz/½ cup butter or margarine, softened

225 g/8 oz/1 cup caster (superfine) sugar

3 eggs, separated

225 g/8 oz/2 cups plain (all-purpose) flour

A pinch of salt

120 ml/4 fl oz/½ cup milk, plus a little extra

5 ml/1 tsp cream of tartar

2.5 ml/½ tsp bicarbonate of soda (baking soda)

A few drops of lemon essence (extract)

A few drops of red food colouring

10 ml/2 tsp cocoa (unsweetened chocolate) powder

For the filling and icing (frosting):

225 g/8 oz/11/3 cups icing (confectioners') sugar, sifted

50 g/2 oz/¼ cup butter or margarine, softened

10 ml/2 tsp hot water

5 ml/1 tsp milk

2.5 ml/½ tsp vanilla essence (extract)

Coloured sugar strands to decorate

To make the cake, cream together the butter or margarine and sugar until light and fluffy. Gradually beat in the egg yolks, then fold in the flour and salt alternately with the milk. Mix the cream of tartar and bicarbonate of soda with a little extra milk, then stir into the mixture. Whisk the egg whites until stiff, then fold into the mixture using a metal spoon. Divide the mixture into three equal portions. Stir the lemon essence into the first bowl, the red food colouring into the second bowl, and the cocoa into the third bowl. Spoon the mixtures into greased and lined 18 cm/7 in cake tins (pans) and bake in a preheated oven at 180°C/ 350°F/gas mark 4 for 25 minutes until golden brown and springy to the touch. Leave to cool in the tins for 5 minutes, then turn out on to a wire rack to finish cooling.

To make the icing, place the icing sugar in a bowl and make a well in the centre. Gradually beat in the butter or margarine, water, milk and vanilla essence until you have a spreadable mixture. Sandwich together the cakes with one-third of the mixture, then spread the remainder over the top and sides of the cake, roughing up the surface with a fork. Sprinkle with top with coloured sugar strands.

Gâteau St-Honoré

Makes one 25 cm/10 in cake

For the choux pastry (paste):
50 g/2 oz/¼ cup unsalted (sweet) butter or margarine

150 ml/¼ pt/2/3 cup milk

A pinch of salt

50 g/2 oz/½ cup plain (all-purpose) flour

2 eggs, lightly beaten

225 g/8 oz Puff Pastry

1 egg yolk

For the caramel:
225 g/6 oz/¾ cup caster (superfine) sugar

90 ml/6 tbsp water

For the filling and decoration:
5 ml/1 tsp powdered gelatine

15 ml/1 tbsp water

1 quantity Vanilla Cream Icing

3 egg whites

175 g/6 oz/¾ cup caster (superfine) sugar

90 ml/6 tbsp water

To make the choux pastry (paste), melt the butter with the milk and salt over a low heat. Bring rapidly to the boil, then remove from the heat and quickly stir in the flour and mix just until the pastry comes away from the sides of the pan. Leave to cool slightly, then very gradually beat in the eggs and continue to beat until smooth and glossy.

108

Roll out the puff pastry to a 26 cm/ 10½ in circle, place on a greased baking (cookie) sheet and prick with a fork. Transfer the choux pastry to a piping bag with a plain 1 cm/½ in nozzle (tip) and pipe a circle round the edge of the puff pastry. Pipe a second circle half-way in towards the centre. On a separate greased baking sheet, pipe the remaining choux pastry into small balls. Brush all the pastry with egg yolk and bake in a preheated oven at 220°C/425°F/gas mark 7 for 12 minutes for the choux balls and 20 minutes for the base until golden and puffed.

To make the caramel, dissolve the sugar in the water, then boil without stirring for about 8 minutes to 160°C/ 320°F until you have a light caramel. Brush the outside ring with caramel, a little at a time. Dip the top half of the balls into the caramel, then press them on to the outside pastry ring.

To make the filling, sprinkle the gelatine over the water in a bowl and leave until spongy. Stand the bowl in a pan of hot water and leave until dissolved. Leave to cool slightly, then stir in the vanilla cream. Whisk the egg whites until stiff. Meanwhile, boil the sugar and water to 120°C/250°F or until a drop in cold water forms a hard ball. Gradually whisk into the egg whites, then continue to whisk until cool. Stir into the custard. Pipe the custard into the centre of the cake and chill before serving.

Strawberry Choux Gâteau

Makes one 23 cm/9 in cake

50 g/2 oz/¼ cup butter or margarine

150 ml/¼ pt/2/3 cup water

75 g/3 oz/1/3 cup plain (all-purpose) flour

A pinch of salt

2 eggs, lightly beaten

50 g/2 oz/1/3 cup icing (confectioners') sugar, sifted

300 ml/½ pt/1¼ cups double (heavy) cream, whipped

225 g/8 oz strawberries, halved

25 g/1 oz/¼ cup flaked (slivered) almonds

Place the butter or margarine and water in a pan and bring slowly to the boil. Remove from the heat and quickly beat in the flour and salt. Gradually beat in the eggs until the dough is shiny and comes away from the sides of the pan. Place spoonfuls of the mixture in a circle on a greased baking (cookie) sheet to build up a circular ring cake and bake in a preheated oven at 220°C/425°F/gas mark 7 for 30 minutes until golden. Leave to cool. Slice the cake in half horizontally. Beat the icing sugar into the cream. Sandwich the halves together with the cream, strawberries and almonds.

Strawberry Fruit Gâteau

Makes one 20 cm/8 in cake

1 cooking (tart) apple, peeled, cored and chopped

25 g/1 oz/3 tbsp dried figs, chopped

25 g/1 oz/3 tbsp raisins

75 g/3 oz/1/3 cup butter or margarine

2 eggs

175 g/6 oz/1½ cups plain (all-purpose) flour

5 ml/1 tsp baking powder

30 ml/2 tbsp milk

225 g/8 oz strawberries, sliced

225 g/8 oz/1 cup fromage frais

Purée the apples, figs, raisins and butter or margarine until light and fluffy. Beat in the eggs, then fold in the flour, baking powder and enough of the milk to mix to a soft dough. Spoon into a greased 20 cm/8 in loose-bottomed cake tin (pan) and bake in a preheated oven at 180°C/ 350°F/gas mark 4 for 30 minutes until firm to the touch. Remove from the tin and leave to cool. Cut the cake in half horizontally. Sandwich together with the strawberries and fromage frais.

Spanish Malaga-soaked Cake

Makes one 23 cm/9 in cake

8 eggs

700 g/1½ lb/3 cups granulated sugar

350 g/12 oz/3 cups plain (all-purpose) flour

300 ml/½ pt/1¼ cups water

350 g/12 oz/1½ cups soft brown sugar

400 ml/14 fl oz/1¾ cups Malaga or fortified wine

Ground cinnamon

Beat the eggs and half the granulated sugar in a heatproof bowl set over a pan of gently simmering water until a thick syrup forms. Gradually add flour, whisking continuously. Spoon into a greased and floured 23 cm/9 in square cake tin (pan) and bake in a preheated oven at 190°C/375°F/gas mark 5 for 45 minutes until springy to the touch. Leave to cool in the tin for 5 minutes before turning out on to a wire rack to finish cooling.

Meanwhile, heat the water in a pan and add the remaining granulated sugar and the brown sugar. Simmer over a medium heat for about 25 minutes until you have a clear, thick syrup. Remove from the heat and leave to cool. Thoroughly mix in the Malaga or wine. Pour the syrup over the cake and serve sprinkled with cinnamon.

Christmas Cake

Makes one 23 cm/9 in cake

350 g/12 oz/1½ cups butter or margarine, softened

350 g/12 oz/1½ cups soft brown sugar

6 eggs

450 g/1 lb/4 cups plain (all-purpose) flour

A pinch of salt

5 ml/1 tsp ground mixed (apple-pie) spice

225 g/8 oz/11/3 cups raisins

450 g/1 lb/22/3 cups sultanas (golden raisins)

225 g/8 oz/11/3 cups currants

175 g/6 oz/1 cup chopped mixed (candied) peel

50 g/2 oz/¼ cup glacé (candied) cherries, chopped

100 g/4 oz/1 cup almonds, chopped

30 ml/2 tbsp black treacle (molasses)

45 ml/3 tbsp brandy

Almond paste

Royal icing

Cream together the butter or margarine and sugar until soft, then beat in the eggs one at a time. Fold in the flour, salt and spice, then mix in all the remaining ingredients. Spoon into a greased and lined 23 cm/9 in cake tin and bake at 140°C/275°F/gas mark 1 for 6½ hours until a skewer inserted in the centre comes out clean. Leave to cool completely, then wrap in foil and store in an airtight container for at least three weeks before covering with almond paste and decorating with royal icing, if liked.

Lightning Source UK Ltd.
Milton Keynes UK
UKHW020657040621
384928UK00011B/756